**Winner
PCM Product
Excellence Award**

W9-BSQ-781

THE ULTIMATE SERGER ANSWER GUIDE

Naomi Baker ◇ Gail Brown
Cindy Kacynski

Troubleshooting
for any
overlock brand
or model

**"This book should come
with every serger
purchased."**

Linda Griepentrog,
Editor, *Sew News* magazine

◆ ◆ ◆ Acknowledgments ◆ ◆ ◆

We are most thankful for the ongoing support generously given by serger companies (for names and addresses, see page 54), sewing-industry vendors (of notions, threads, fabrics, and many more products than space allows us to list here), sewing machine dealers, fabric store owners and their personnel, educators, serger-sewing enthusiasts, and of course, our families.

Other Books by Naomi Baker
(All available from Krause Publications)

* Serged Garments in Minutes, *with Tammy Young*
* Sew Sensational Gifts, *with Tammy Young*
* Serge a Simple Project, *with Tammy Young*
* Distinctive Serger Gifts and Crafts, *with Tammy Young*

Other Books by Gail Brown

* Quick Gifts and Decor, *with Nancy Zieman*
* The All-New Creative Serging Illustrated, *with Sue Green and Pati Palmer*
* Gail Brown's All-New Instant Interiors
* Sewing with Sergers, *with Pati Palmer*
* Creative Serging, *with Sue Green and Pati Palmer*
* Sensational Silk

◆ ◆ ◆

Copyright © 1996 by Naomi Baker, Gail Brown, Cindy Kacynski
Updated 1999
All Rights Reserved

Published by

kp krause publications
An Imprint of F+W Publications

700 East State Street • Iola, WI 54990-0001
715-445-2214 • 888-457-2873
www.krausebooks.com

No part of this book may be reproduced, transmitted, or stored in any form or by any means, electronic or mechanical, without prior written permission from the publisher.

Cover/Interior Design, Photo Styling, and Illustrations by Patty Edwards
Photographs by Rick Kessinger

Manufactured in the United States of America

Library of Congress Cataloging-in-Publication Data

Baker, Naomi.
  The ultimate serger answer guide / Naomi Baker, Gail Brown, Cindy Kacynski.
    p. cm. — (Creative machine arts series)
  Includes bibliographical references and index.
    ISBN 13: 978-0-8019-8645-1 (pbk.)
    ISBN 10: 0-8019-8645-1 (pbk.)
    1. Serging — Handbooks, manuals, etc. 2. Sewing machines — Handbooks, manuals, etc. I. Brown, Gail. II. Kacynski, Cindy.
III. Title. IV. Series.
TT713.B335 1996
646.2'044 — dc20   95-33546
                    CIP

"If you've ever wished a top serging expert could be looking over your shoulder to solve the mystery of that imperfect stitch, your wish has been granted. This easiest-ever troubleshooting guide should be at the hands of all serger owners, offering a sure cure (or several!) to every serging problem. With Naomi, Gail, and Cindy in your sewing room, it will be smooth serging!"

Shirley Adams,
host of "The Sewing
Connection" PBS Series

"The Ultimate Serger Answer Guide is a well-illustrated, user-friendly troubleshooting book. It's perfectly organized to let you quickly and easily identify your problems, solve them, and get on with your project, just as the name implies."

Sandra Betzina, author of
"Power Sewing" books, hostess
of "Sew Perfect" on HGTV

"This book opens all the stops and allows you to play with your serger, worry-free. It addresses every aspect of serger troubleshooting—beyond the usual tension problems—and is organized and cross-referenced so solutions are easy to locate. The Ultimate Serger Answer Guide is a terrific reference book to have near your serger."

Jean Fristensky,
National Director,
The American Sewing Guild

"The Ultimate Serger Answer Guide is definitely not a coffee table book—this comprehensive problem-solver will be as close to the serger as the thread snippers! The authors 'say it like it is' to help identify and resolve common and not-so-common serging problems, exploring the most typical, as well as remote causes. Their years of teaching and serging experience is invaluable. This book should come with every serger purchased—for the sanity of the buyer, as well as the dealer!"

Linda Turner Griepentrog,
Editor, **Sew News** magazine

"The Ultimate Serger Answer Guide is the type of troubleshooting reference serger owners have dreamed about. It categorizes serging problems, then offers clear-cut solutions for each. This practical, reader-friendly book is packed with illustrations, tips, and tricks to maneuver out of any serging dilemma, or prevent potential problems. Whether you're a serging novice or a seasoned veteran, this is an invaluable resource."

Nancy Zieman,
President, Nancy's Notions Ltd.

❖❖❖ Contents ❖❖❖

✦✦✦ Contents ✦✦✦

We've designed this book as an answer guide, organizing information so you can identify your problems and find your solutions. Remember, you don't have to review the pages in sequence; the format and content are modular for fast, easy reference.

◆ Identify your problem. Look in "Contents" under Chapter 1, determining whether the problem is related to the stitch, needle, knife, etc.:

✧ Stitch-Related Problems (pages 8-27)

✧ Needle-Related Problems (pages 28-31)

✧ Knife-Related Problems (pages 32-33)

✧ Seam and Edge Problems (pages 34-41)

✧ Rolled-Edge Problems (pages 42-43)

✧ Flatlocking Problems (pages 44-45)

✧ Decorative Serging Problems (pages 46-49)

For instance, if one or more of your threads continues to break, look under "Stitch-Related Problems," to find "Thread Breakage" on pages 14–15 (A):

(A)

Solutions are listed sequentially, starting with the most likely techniques.

◆ If you can't locate your problem or solutions in Chapter 1, turn to the comprehensive Index (pages 93-95). Identify and locate a term or item relating to the problem. For instance, if you're having difficulty with the thread continually breaking, look under "Thread" to find (B).

(B)

◆ If you need a handy, at-a-glance reference while serging, turn to the "Troubleshooting Chart" (pages 88-89). In addition to summarizing solutions from Chapter 1, this chart (C) incorporates tips from Chapter 2 ("Insider Insights") and Chapter 4 ("Serging Smarts").

(C)

Can't Balance Tensions (pages 8-9)	◆ Turn knobs right to tight ◆ Turn lay-in dials up to tig ◆ Tighten loopy threads, or ◆ Loosen puckered threads
No Stitch Formation (pages 10, 48-49)	◆ Check threading paths. ◆ Confirm needles are fully ◆ Be sure needle type and s

Note: "Insider Insights" (pages 53-64) features tips about specific brands, but most of the information is applicable to all sergers.

◆ If you have questions about buying a serger, which foot or needle to use, thread options and applications, machine maintenance, or mail-order sources, consult Chapter 4.

◆ If you don't find the solution to your particular serging problem, we'd like to know about it for revised editions and new books. Turn to page 96, our reader feedback page. Send us your name, any unanswered questions, and comments about this book; you might win a free one-year subscription to **Sew News** magazine or an "Ultimate Serger Answer Guide" video.

◆ If you are at your wit's end, take a break. Step back from your serging problem for a while. Highly stressed or late-night serging sessions can lead to quagmires that mysteriously vanish when approached with a fresh, rested perspective.

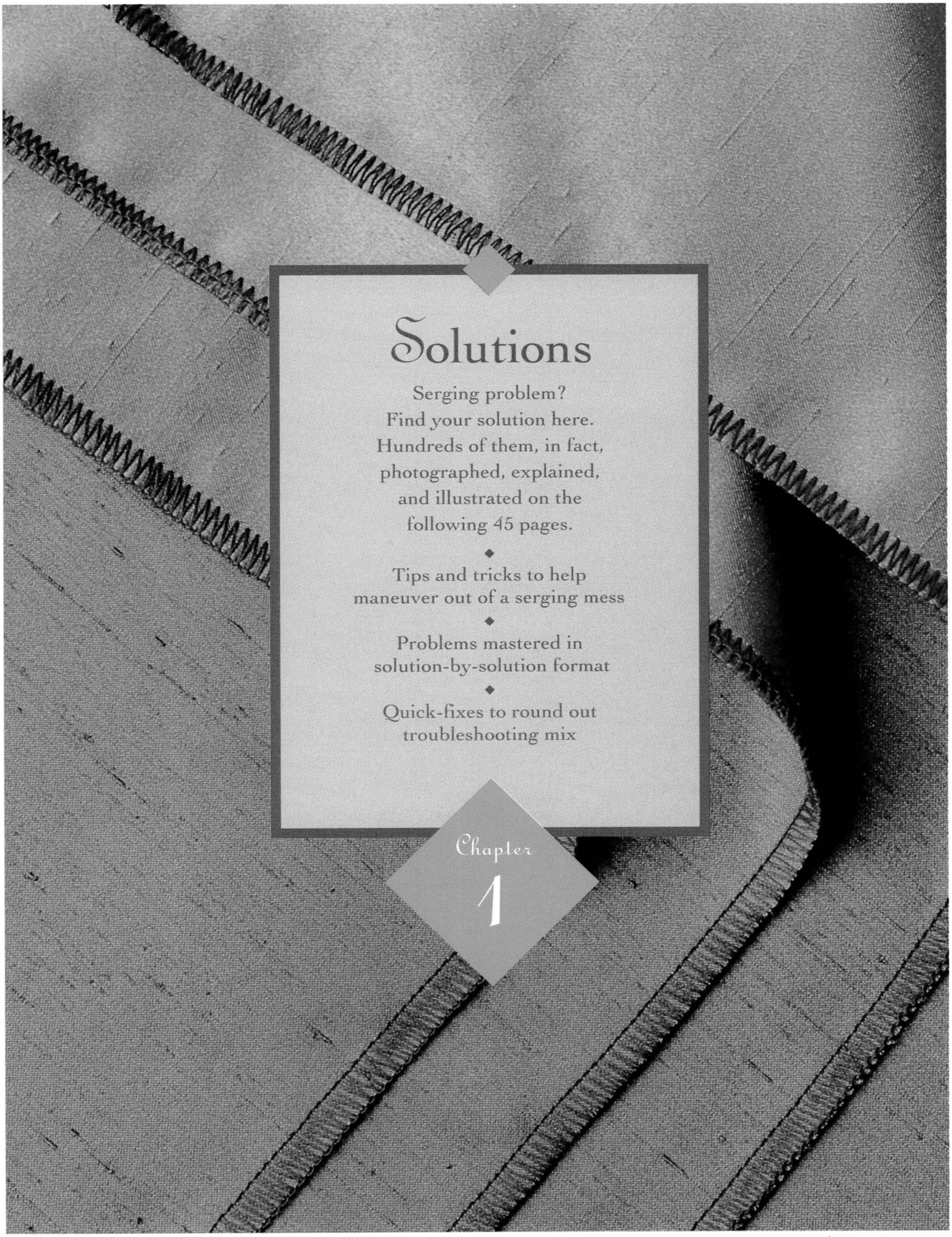

Solutions

Serging problem?
Find your solution here.
Hundreds of them, in fact,
photographed, explained,
and illustrated on the
following 45 pages.

◆

Tips and tricks to help
maneuver out of a serging mess

◆

Problems mastered in
solution-by-solution format

◆

Quick-fixes to round out
troubleshooting mix

Chapter

1

Problem: Can't Balance Tensions

Solutions:

◆ Tension controls (for most, but not all sergers): Knobs—turn right to tighten, left to loosen; lay-in discs—turn up to tighten, down to loosen. Important: Make sure the thread is seated in the tension knob or lay-in disc.

◆ Adjust only one knob or dial at a time; test-serge and assess the results. Make further adjustments if necessary.

◆ Loopy threads indicate too much thread; tighten tensions. To expose more thread, loosen tensions.

◆ To balance the stitch, loosen the tightest tension first.

◆ Understand how stitch, thread, and fabric characteristics affect tension:

◇ Stitch length affects looper tensions. Shortening the stitch loosens looper tensions; lengthening the stitch tightens looper tensions.

◇ Stitch width affects looper tensions. Narrowing the stitch loosens looper tensions. Widening the stitch tightens looper tensions.

◇ Thread type affects tension. Heavier threads take up more room in the tension controls; loosen to balance tensions. Stretchy threads, such as woolly stretch nylon or monofilament-nylon, stretch as they pass through the guides, tightening tension; loosen to balance tensions.

◇ Fabric weight affects tension. Heavier fabrics require more thread for coverage; loosen tensions. Lightweight fabrics require less thread for coverage; tighten tensions.

Balanced and Irregular 2-Thread Overedge Tensions

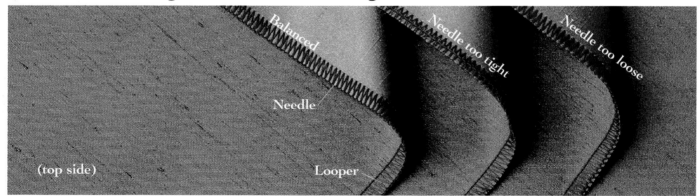

Shown above: *With balanced tensions (left sample), the needle thread looks like straight stitching on the top side and interlocks with the looper thread on the edge.*

Balanced and Irregular 2-Thread Chainstitch Tensions

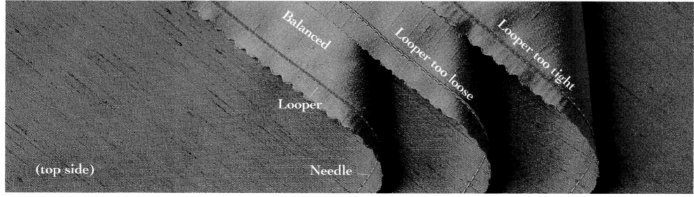

Shown above: *With balanced tensions (left sample), the needle thread looks like straight stitching on the top side, and the needle and looper threads interlock in a chain configuration on the underside.*

Balanced and Irregular 3-Thread Overlock Tensions

Shown above: *With balanced tensions (left sample), the upper and lower looper threads interlock at the edge. The needle thread looks like straight stitching on the top side and tiny loops of thread on the underside.*

Balanced and Irregular 3/4-Thread Overlock Tensions

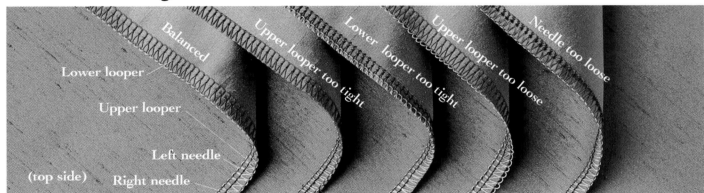

Shown above: *With balanced tensions (left sample), the upper and lower looper threads interlock at the edge. The needle threads look like two rows of straight stitching on the top side and two rows of tiny loops of thread on the underside.*

Balanced and Irregular 3-Thread Cover Hem/Stitch Tensions

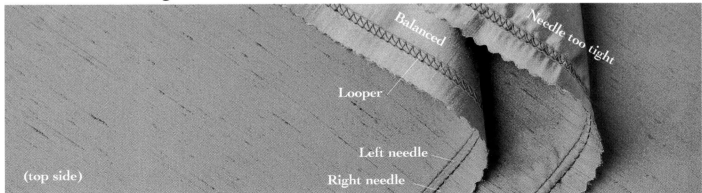

Shown above: *With balanced tensions (left sample), the needle threads look like two rows of straight stitching on the top side, and the looper thread interlocks back and forth between the needle threads on the underside.*

Note: 4-thread and 5-thread stitches not pictured here are composites of the stitches shown (see pages 66-67).

Problem: No Stitch Formation

Solutions:

◆ Troubleshoot threading paths (A). Make sure needles and loopers are threaded through all respective tension discs or dials, guides, and—most important—the eyes.

(A) Troubleshoot threading

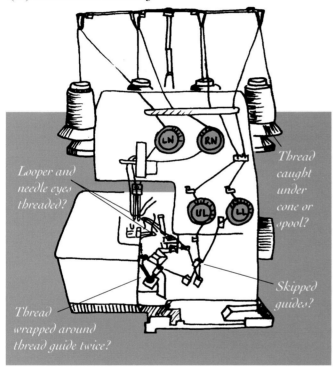

Looper and needle eyes threaded?

Thread caught under cone or spool?

Skipped guides?

Thread wrapped around thread guide twice?

◆ Confirm that the needle is fully inserted into the needle-clamp slot (see pages 28-29).

◆ Be certain you're using the correct needle type. (See page 84.) If the serger requires industrial needles and you're using household needles (or vice versa), a stitch usually won't form. Also, if your model uses industrial needles, use the correct type (DCx1, BLx1, DBx1, JLx1—see page 84).

◆ Position needles properly: eye directly to the front, groove to the front, scarf to the back (see pages 28-29).

◆ Replace bent or burred needles.

◆ Lower the presser foot. Some sergers, and particularly those with a tension-release feature, cannot form a stitch with the presser foot up.

◆ Place all threads under the presser foot when starting to serge, and pull on the thread tails gently to help advance the stitch (B).

(B) Gently pull thread chain to advance stitch.

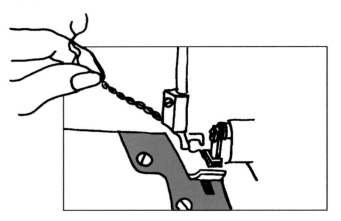

◆ Rethread with softer, finer, and/or more tightly plied looper threads. Some threads are too stiff, thick, and/or loosely plied to form a loop around the needle thread, and so a stitch cannot be formed.

My Solutions:

Problem: Irregular Stitch Formation

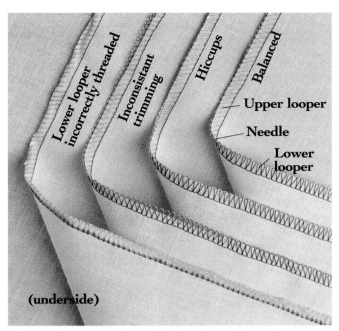

Shown above: *Irregular and balanced serged samples.*

Solutions:

◆ Check the threading paths (refer to the illustration in your manual), asking these questions:

⬧ Have any guides been missed?

⬧ Is the telescopic thread guide fully extended?

⬧ Are the threads seated in the tension controls?

⬧ Is the thread stand set up and positioned correctly?

⬧ Are the thread paths completely unobstructed?

(Anything pushing against the threads will alter the tension and cause irregularities.)

◆ Balance the tensions (see pages 8-9).

◆ Replace the needle and position it properly. Depending on the serger model and fabric, you may need a different needle size or type to ensure stitch uniformity (see pages 28-29, 84).

◆ Trim evenly while serging, or maintain an even distance from the fabric edge or fold. (The fabric within the looper threads holds the stitch width.)

◆ Confirm that the thread is feeding smoothly and consistently. Utilize thread nets and spool caps (A) if catching in the notch is a problem. Also, scratch off any label glue on the spool or cone.

(A) *Smooth serging*

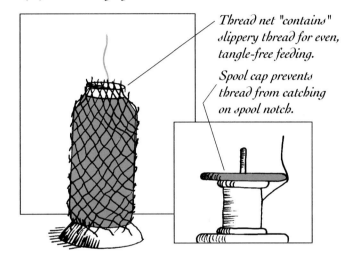

Thread net "contains" slippery thread for even, tangle-free feeding.

Spool cap prevents thread from catching on spool notch.

◆ Lengthen the stitch slightly.

◆ Tighten tensions slightly. First tighten the loopers, then, if needed, the needle.

◆ Change threads. Old, poor-quality, or intensely dyed threads may be causing stitch irregularities.

◆ Sand off fine burrs on the loopers or throat plate (see page 90).

My Solutions:

Problem: Can't Rethread

Solutions:

◆ Serger already threaded? Try the tie-on method (A).

(A)

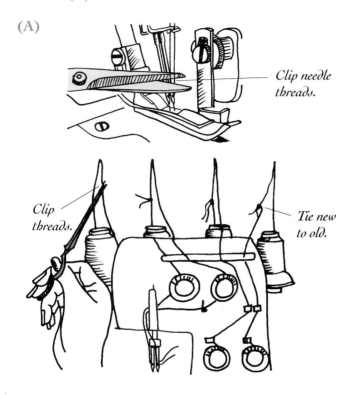

Clip needle threads.

Clip threads.

Tie new to old.

1. Clip the needle thread just above needle eye.

2. Clip all threads close to the cones or spools on the thread pins. Remove the cones or spools and replace with the new threads. Using square or overhand knots (see page 61), tie to the threads currently on the machine.

3. Completely loosen all tension controls or remove threads from each tension knob or disc. Or, if your machine has the feature, activate tension-release.

4. Carefully pull each thread through the serger, one at a time. After trimming off the knot, rethread the needle. Return to normal tension settings, or replace the threads in the tension knobs or discs. Holding the thread above and below the tension discs, give it a tug to make sure it is seated (see page 57); repeat for each thread.

◆ Before serging, place all the thread tails under and to the left of the foot. When you start to serge, gently pull on the tails to advance the stitch.

◆ If your serger is unthreaded, refer to your manual. Photocopy (preferably enlarge), and use colored felt-tip pens to trace the threading paths, coordinating the ink colors to your serger's color-coded threading guides. Start threading in the specified sequence, generally (but not always) from right to left, or from the lower looper to the needles (B).

(B) *Common threading sequence*—right to left:*

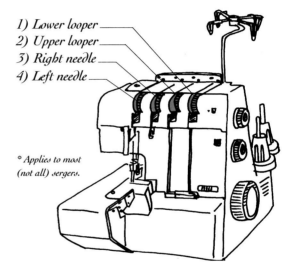

1) *Lower looper*
2) *Upper looper*
3) *Right needle*
4) *Left needle*

* *Applies to most (not all) sergers.*

◆ Put handy notions to work when threading. Serger tweezers maneuver thread strands through guide openings and looper/needle eyes (see page 73). Looper threaders dramatically enhance accessibility to the looper guides and eyes (see page 75). Simple needle threaders can instantly thread any strand through looper and needle eyes (see pages 59, 75).

My Solutions:

Problem: 2- and 3-Thread Conversions

Solutions:

◆ Check to make sure your model will convert to 2-thread serging (not all models do). Consult your manual; if still uncertain, ask your dealer.

On models that feature 2-thread conversion, the upper looper eye accommodates the converter (built in or accessory). This allows the upper looper to carry the lower looper thread over the top of the fabric to interlock with the needle thread.

Note: Although the stitches look the same, 2/4-thread and rare 2-thread models are configured differently than models that convert to 2-thread serging. On a 2/4- or 2-thread machine, the upper looper (or looper) interlocks with the needle thread. No conversion is necessary, and it won't adjust for 3-thread serging.

◆ If available, refer to the 3- to 2-thread conversion steps printed in your manual and/or on the inside of your serger's looper cover. Or follow these steps:

1. Clip the upper looper thread just below the tension control (you will not be using the upper looper eye).

2. Turn the handwheel until the upper looper is to the right of the needle (or as instructed in your manual).

3. Push the converter to the left (or attach the converter

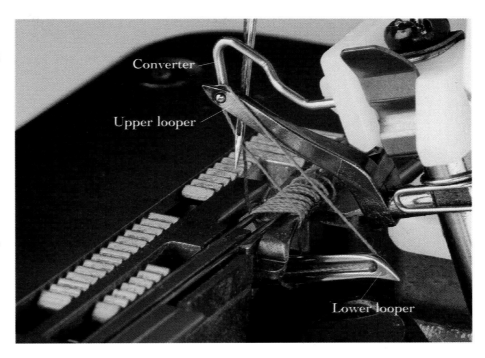

Converter

Upper looper

Lower looper

accessory) so the tiny hook catches in the upper looper eye (A). If the needle and lower looper are threaded, the machine is set up for 2-thread serging. Loosen the needle tension as necessary to balance the tension (see page 8).

(A) *Converter*

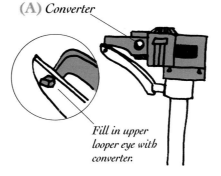

Fill in upper looper eye with converter.

◆ To return to 3-thread serging (also refer to your manual):

1. Turn the handwheel until the upper looper is above the lower looper.

2. Disengage the converter by slipping the hook out of the looper's eye, and to the right. Or remove the converter accessory.

3. Rethread the upper looper and readjust the needle tension (may require tightening).

My Solutions:

Problem: Thread Breakage

Solutions:

◆ Loosen tensions incrementally, starting with the thread that breaks most frequently, and/or the tightest tension.

◆ Thoroughly inspect the threading paths **(A)**. Are threads caught or tangled on spools or cones, thread rods, or guides? Is the telescopic thread guide in its fully extended position? Is the needle thread going directly through the eye, or is it possibly wrapped around the needle?

(A) *Inspect threading paths:*

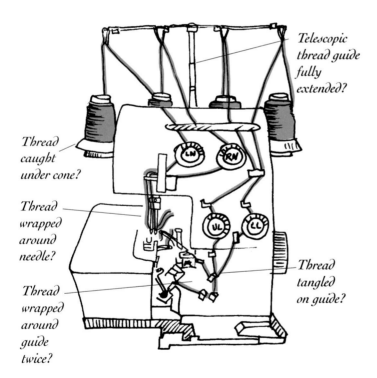

Telescopic thread guide fully extended?

Thread caught under cone?

Thread wrapped around needle?

Thread wrapped around guide twice?

Thread tangled on guide?

◆ Rethread from scratch, following the correct threading sequence described in your manual (see page 12). Finish by threading the needle. Before starting to serge, all thread tails should be above the throat plate.

◆ If the lower looper thread keeps breaking, it's likely caused by out-of-sequence threading. For example, if the lower looper is threaded after the needle (likely the most accessible needle-down position), the needle thread will be trapped under the looper. As the stitch advances, the needle thread pulls up on the lower looper and the thread breaks **(B)**.

(B) *Problem: Needle threads trapped under lower looper.*

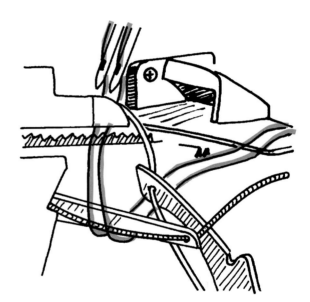

To prevent this problem from recurring, simply rethread the needle after threading the lower looper. Or, rather than rethreading, use tweezers to draw up the needle thread tail above the throat plate after threading the lower looper **(C)**.

(C) *Solution: Rethread needles or draw up needle threads.*

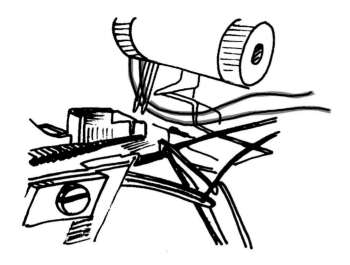

◆ Place all thread tails under and to the left of the foot. Gently pull the tails when starting to serge.

◆ Change to a new needle. The needle you're using may be bent, burred, or the wrong size or type. For needle threads that break persistently, try a larger-eyed needle, such as a jeans, topstitching, Metalfil, or Schmetz Machine Embroidery, if appropriate for your serger model (see page 84).

◆ Test for burrs on the looper tips and eyes, the needle eye, and the throat plate: Run a strand of woolly stretch nylon over the area and watch for catching or shredding of the thread (indicative of burrs).

If you feel burrs on the needle eye, replace the needle. If you feel burrs on the loopers and/or throat plate, try to lightly sand them off using crocus cloth (see page 74); if the burrs remain, consult your dealer.

◆ Replace your thread with a new, name-brand thread. Old or poor-quality threads can break easily when subjected to the rigors and speed of serging.

◆ Use thread nets (see page 19) if thread is falling off the spools or cones and catching on the thread pins.

◆ Use spool caps (see page 19) to prevent threads from catching on the notches of all-purpose spools.

◆ If your lower looper is self-threading, make certain it was returned to its correct position for serging (not the position for threading).

◆ Troubleshoot thread breakage when chainstitching: Lengthen the stitch to at least 2.5mm, and start stitching on fabric, not "air" (also refer to page 24).

My Solutions:

Problem: Hairy Edges

Hairy edge

Shortened stitch

Thicker looper thread

Double-stitched

Consistent grain

(top side)

Shown above: Some remedies for hairy edges include shortening the stitch length, using thicker looper threads, serging the edge twice, and/or serge-finishing a consistent grainline.

Solutions:

◆ Allow the serger knives to trim the edge at least slightly. Doing so will neaten ragged or fraying edges.

◆ Shorten the stitch length. Increased thread coverage will help hide straying fibers (see photo).

◆ Change to a thicker or multifilament (such as woolly stretch nylon) thread in the looper(s). Increased thread coverage discourages unruly fabric hairs (see photo).

◆ Reposition or change lower knife. It may be out of alignment or dull, causing ragged cutting (see pages 32-33).

◆ Before serging, sparingly apply seam sealant along the trimming line. (For the finest line of sealant, transfer with a pin or toothpick tip.) Allow to dry before stitching. The seam sealant stiffens the fabric and seals the edge, resulting in clean, even cutting and fewer fiber hairs escaping through the stitches (A).

(A) Apply seam sealant along the trimming line:

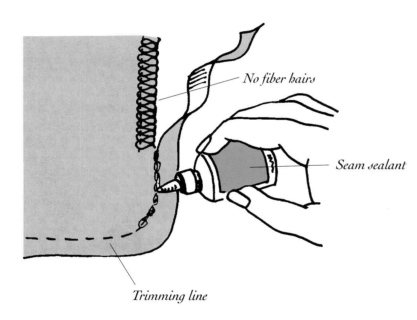

No fiber hairs

Seam sealant

Trimming line

◆ Serge over the edge twice. Before serging the second row, readjust your serger for a slightly wider, shorter stitch. Serge directly over the first row, positioning the finished edge just to the left of the knife (take care not to cut the stitches—see photo on page 16).

◆ If using a rolled or wrapped stitch (see pages 66-67), change to a balanced-tension stitch (see pages 8-9). Fibers are less likely to poke out of a stitch that interlocks at the edge than one that wraps.

◆ Stabilize the underside of the edge before serging. To create a more consistently even, stable edge, use lightweight fusible interfacing or another layer of stable, thin fabric on the underside.

◆ If possible, recut the edge so the grain is consistent—i.e., is all-lengthwise, all-crosswise, or all-bias. Different grainlines finish differently, and some are particularly prone to producing hairy edges. Random and crosswise grainlines on certain fabrics can be especially problematic, whereas true lengthwise grainlines usually serge-finish very neatly (see photo on page 16).

◆ If your rolled edge is hairy, try increasing the stitch width or bite (consult your manual for this adjustment). More fabric will be rolled under the stitch, preventing fibers from poking out between the threads.

◆ Another remedy for a hairy rolled edge: Serge over a layer of water-soluble stabilizer (see page 42). The stabilizer will effectively roll loose fibers inside the stitch (a real lifesaver when working with wiry metallic fabrics). For more rolled-edge solutions, see pages 42-43.

◆ If all else fails, cheat. Simply use sharp, small scissors to trim peekaboo fibers. Or "train" loose fibers with seam sealant, such as Fray Check™ or No-Fray™; apply sparingly to the edge and when tacky, roll the threads under, hiding them in the stitch.

My Solutions:

Problem: Skipped Stitches

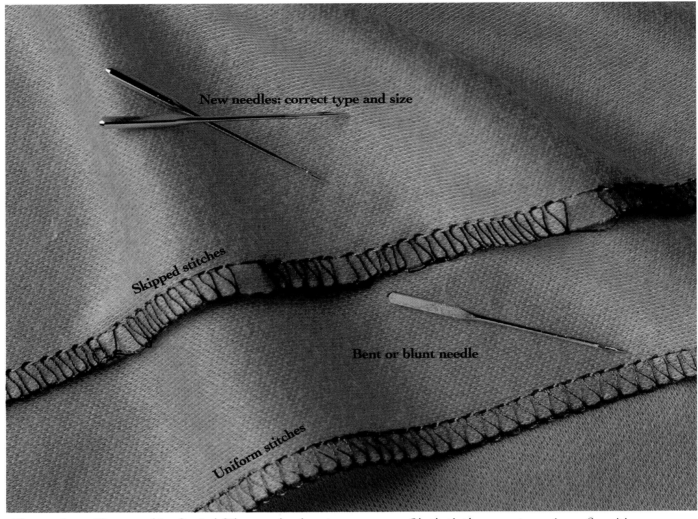

New needles: correct type and size

Skipped stitches

Bent or blunt needle

Uniform stitches

Shown above: *Fix most skipped-stitch dilemmas by changing to a new needle that's the proper type, size, and position.*

Solutions:

◆ Visually trace threading paths for accuracy. Make sure you've threaded all respective tension discs or dials, guides, and eyes. Also, be sure the telescopic thread guide is fully extended.

◆ If serging knits, use a stretch or ballpoint needle (see page 84), which will prevent both skipped stitches and tearing of the fabric fibers.

◆ Change to a new needle (yours could be bent, burred, or blunt; see page 84). When inserting the new needle, make sure it's positioned properly and pushed all the way up into the needle-clamp slot (see pages 28-29).

◆ Loosen the tightest tension. The thread may be too tight to consistently interlock with the other thread(s), causing skipping.

◆ If skipping remains a problem—even after changing the needle—try replacing it with a new, different-sized needle (usually one size larger, but make sure it's within the recommended size range). Also, consult your dealer or the manufacturer about a needle suitable for your model that's specially designed to prevent skipped stitches (such as Organ HAX1SP and the Schmetz ELx705; see page 84).

(A) *Smooth serging*

◆ Confirm that the thread is feeding smoothly and consistently. Utilize thread nets and spool caps (A) if catching in the notch or on the machine is a problem.

◆ If using heavier fabric, try increasing the presser foot pressure (see page 70). Doing so will allow the feed dogs to advance the fabric more uniformly.

◆ Serge over a strip of water-soluble stabilizer, which will stabilize and smooth the edge, minimizing skipped stitches. (The stabilizer will dissolve during the first laundering.) Or stabilize the edge before serging with lightweight fusible interfacing, or another layer of stable, thin fabric or trim.

◆ Start over, completely rethreading your serger.

◆ If all these solutions have been tried and skipped stitches persist, consult your dealer. Your serger's timing could be off and require servicing.

My Solutions:

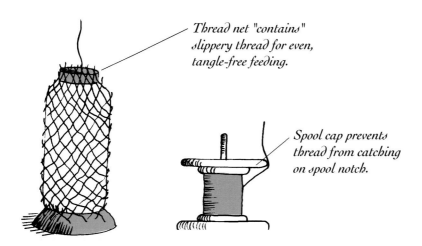

Thread net "contains" slippery thread for even, tangle-free feeding.

Spool cap prevents thread from catching on spool notch.

◆ Watch for label glue on the thread spool or cone. Remove by scratching or winding off, or dissolving with rubbing alcohol. Rethread with a quality, name-brand thread (preferably new), starting with the loopers, then the needles.

◆ Prewash your fabric to remove finishes that resist stitch penetration.

◆ Practice taut-serging (see page 35).

◆ Clean the needle after serging through glue-backed fabric or trim, or fusible webs. (The residue can hamper stitch formation.) Apply rubbing alcohol or needle lubricant on a soft cloth and gently wipe needle surfaces.

Problem: Stitch Isn't Wide Enough

Stitch not as wide as desired

Loosened upper looper

Shortened stitch

Stabilized edge

(top side)

Shown above: *Widen serged stitches and correct tunneling (allowing the fabric to lie flat within the looper threads) by loosening the upper looper thread tension, shortening the stitch length, and/or stabilizing the edge before serging.*

Solutions:

◆ Widen stitch width or bite (A, page 21) using the dial, lever, or a screwdriver to move the lower knife to the right (consult your manual).

◆ Use the left needle of 3/4-thread stitch (see pages 66-67). The farther the needle is from the knife, the wider the stitch.

◆ Be certain you're using the correct foot and/or plate. Some models require changing the foot and/or plate with a wider stitch finger. The stitch is formed over the finger; the wider the finger, the wider the stitch.

(A) *Cutting width: Move lower knife blade right to widen.*

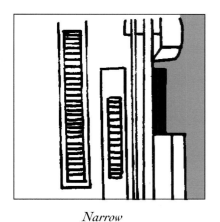

Narrow

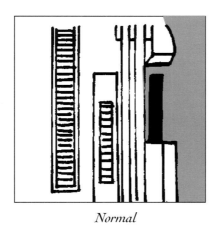

Normal

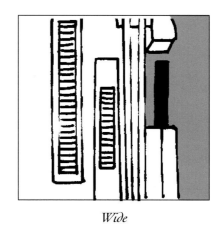

Wide

◆ Loosen looper tensions. The looser the looper tension, the more thread that is laid down, and hence, the wider the stitch. Conversely, as the looper tension is tightened, the stitch is narrowed.

◆ When using heavy, decorative threads in the loopers, simply loosening the tension control may not be adequate. If more loosening is required, remove the threads in the following order, test-serging after each to assess if the tension is loose enough (see pages 48-49):

1. Remove the decorative thread from the first guide above the tension control. If the tension is still too tight...

2. Remove the decorative thread from one or more of the lower (below the tension control) guides. If the tension is still too tight...

3. Remove the decorative thread from the actual tension dial or disc (see page 49).

◆ Shorten the stitch length to allow for looser looper tensions.

◆ Change to thicker looper thread. The thicker thread will create a beefier, wider stitch.

◆ Recheck threading, particularly the loopers. Thread may be caught on guides, thread pins, or spool notches.

◆ Remove thread nets; they tighten the thread tensions, thus narrowing the stitch.

◆ Before serging, stabilize the edge with fusible interfacing or another layer of lightweight fabric or trim.

◆ Use a more stable fabric. Soft fabrics can collapse under the stitch, causing the stitch to narrow. (That's why many serged-stitch demonstrations are done on starched batiste—a very uniform, stiff fabric that holds the width of the stitch.)

My Solutions:

Problem: Stitch Isn't Narrow Enough

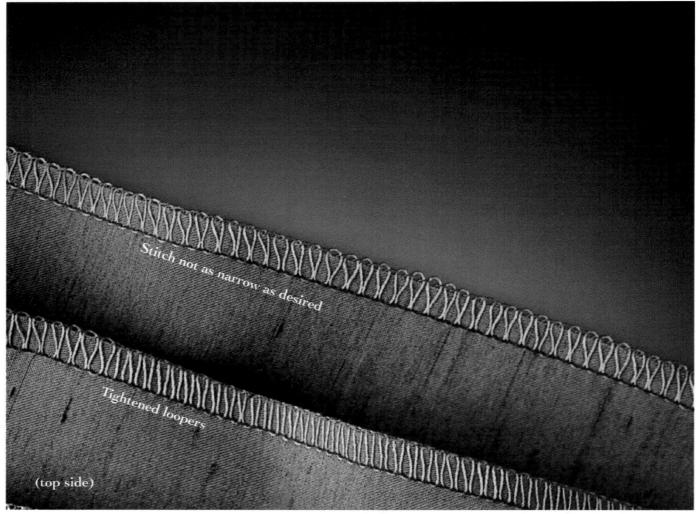

Stitch not as narrow as desired

Tightened loopers

(top side)

Shown above and right: *To narrow serged stitches—snugging thread loops to the fabric edge—tighten the looper tensions, use finer looper thread, and/or lengthen the stitch.*

Solutions:

◆ Narrow the stitch width or bite. Consult your manual. This may involve using the dial, lever, or a screwdriver to move the lower knife to the left.

◆ Use the right needle of 3/4-thread stitch. The closer the needle is to the knife, the narrower the stitch.

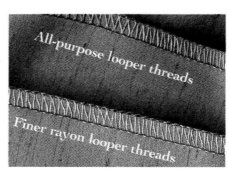

All-purpose looper threads

Finer rayon looper threads

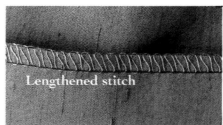

Lengthened stitch

◆ Be certain you're using the correct foot and/or plate. Some models require changing to a foot and/or plate with a narrower stitch finger (A). The stitch is formed over the finger; the narrower the finger, the narrower the stitch.

(A)

For medium width: standard stitch finger

For narrow width: narrow stitch finger

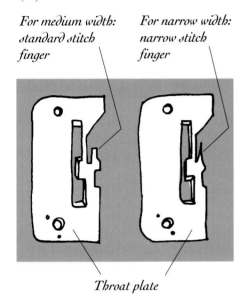

Throat plate

Note: For the narrowest seaming and finishing, consider changing to the rolled edge foot and/or plate (and the rolled-edge needle position), even if using a balanced tension.

◆ Tighten the looper tensions. The tighter the looper tension, the less thread that is laid down, and hence, the narrower the

stitch (see photo on page 22). Conversely, as the looper tension is loosened, the stitch is widened.

◆ Rethread the loopers with a stretchy thread, such as woolly stretch nylon (see page 86) to further increase tension-tightening. This multifilament thread stretches as it passes through the guides and eyes, further tightening the looper tensions.

◆ Rethread the loopers with a finer thread. The fine thread will create a narrower stitch (see photo on page 22).

◆ Use a softer and/or thinner fabric. Or prewash your fabric to soften the finish. Soft fabrics collapse under the stitch, causing the stitch to narrow.

◆ Practice other looper-tension-tightening (and stitch narrowing) strategies:

    ◇ Lengthen the stitch length to allow for tighter looper tensions (see lower right photo on page 22).

    ◇ Recheck threading, particularly the loopers.

◇ Make sure the threads are completely seated in the tension controls.

◇ Pull the telescopic thread guide to its fully extended position.

My Solutions:

Problem: Chainstitch Won't Form, or Breaks

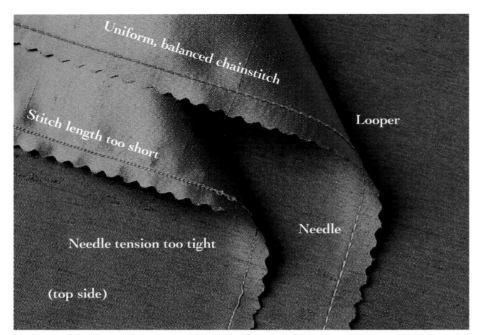

Uniform, balanced chainstitch

Stitch length too short

Looper

Needle

Needle tension too tight

(top side)

Shown above: *Lengthen the stitch and loosen the needle tension to prevent breakage.*

Solutions:

To facilitate chainstitch formation:

◆ Make sure the chainstitch needle (not on all sergers) is inserted and inserted properly: eye and groove directly to the front, groove to the front, scarf to the back **(A)**. The chainstitch needle is located to the left of, lower, and in front of the other needle positions.

◆ Balance the tensions (see page 8).

◆ Be sure the chainstitch needle and chainstitch looper guides and eyes are threaded properly (refer to your manual.)

Also make certain the telescopic thread guide is fully extended, and that the threads are seated in the tension controls.

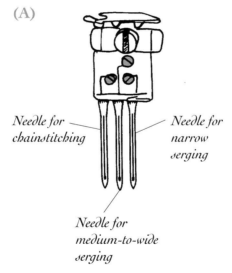

(A)

Needle for chainstitching

Needle for narrow serging

Needle for medium-to-wide serging

*(**Note:** Three needles are used simultaneously only for triple-needle coverstitching.)*

To prevent chainstitch breakage:

◆ Loosen the needle tension, and balance with the chainstitch looper tension. See page 8.

◆ Lengthen the stitch to at least 2.5mm.

◆ Don't serge "on air." Start chainstitching on fabric, with the presser foot down.

◆ Use the correct foot and/or throat plate.

◆ Start serging with the needle thread completely above the throat plate **(B)**, or above the foot (check your manual).

(B) *Start with threads above throat plate.*

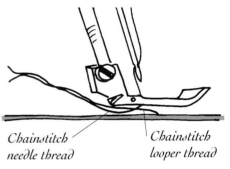

Chainstitch needle thread

Chainstitch looper thread

◆ Check the threading paths. If you rethread the chainstitch looper, do so before rethreading the needle. (This will prevent the needle thread from being trapped underneath the chainstitch looper thread.)

◆ Replace the needle if damaged (see pages 28-29).

My Solutions:

Problem: Clicking, Excessive Noise

Solutions:

◆ Visually trace threading paths, watching for missed guides. Also, watch for thread wrapped around (rather than through) guides, caught in spool notches, or trapped under spools or cones on thread pins.

◆ If it's a distinctive clicking noise, the needle may be hitting the lower looper. Check by removing the needle and running the machine, listening for the same noises. If quieted, try properly inserting a new needle (see pages 28-29) and running the machine again.

◆ If removing or replacing the needle doesn't eliminate a clicking noise, call your dealer. Your serger may have timing problems or a bent looper.

◆ Replace the needle with a smaller size (do not use larger than a size 14/90).

◆ Change to a new needle. Yours could be bent, burred, or blunt.

◆ Make sure the upper and lower knife blades are in their correct positions. (The upper knife must butt against the lower knife in order to cut.) Consult your manual for proper alignment.

◆ Inspect the upper knife blade. If it's worn, damaged, or out of alignment, it may need to be replaced. Call your dealer for an upper knife replacement (most are not supplied as a standard accessory) and an installation estimate (you may opt to replace it yourself).

◆ Move the looper threader to the correct position, if applicable.

(A) Pad stabilizes serger and absorbs noise.

Stabilizing/silencing pad

◆ Clean and oil your serger (see page 90).

◆ Loosen your tightest tensions, one thread at a time. Try serging after each adjustment to gauge if loosening reduces the noise.

◆ Work on a stable surface. Flimsy card tables or TV trays contribute to vibration and noise.

◆ To reduce noise and vibration place the serger on a stabilizing/silencing pad (A). Use one specially designed for sergers, or adapt a computer mouse pad or printer pad (trim to custom-fit the footprint of your serger model).

My Solutions:

Problem: Machine Jams

Solutions:

◆ Stop! Don't continue to press on the foot pedal if the machine is jammed. Cut away any thread or fabric wrapped around the stitch finger or loopers. (Try clipping threads first; if that doesn't free the jam, then clip the fabric.) Finally, test for unhampered stitch formation by turning the handwheel manually, rather than pressing on the foot pedal.

◆ If the needle is out of the fabric, raise the needle bar to its highest position and remove the foot. If possible, disengage the knives. Carefully try to pull the jammed threads and fabric to the back, slipping them off the stitch finger (A). Replace the foot, rethread as necessary, and engage the knives.

(A) *Remove foot, raise knife (if possible), pull jam off stitch finger.*

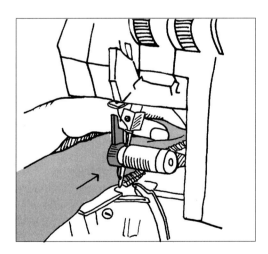

◆ If the needle is trapped in the jam, loosen the set-screw and raise the needle bar to the highest position. Pull out the needle(s), or allow it to drop through. Then remove the foot, and if possible, disengage the knives. Cut away the threads wrapped around the jam (possibly under the lower looper), so you can pull the stitches and fabric off the stitch finger. Replace the foot and the needle, rethread as necessary, and engage the knives.

Note: Replace your needle if it has been bent or blunted in the jam.

◆ Check all precautions (mentioned below and on page 27) before proceeding.

◆ Prevent jams before they happen:

✧ Always serge with the looper cover closed (B). With the cover open, fabrics and threads can get caught in the loopers, causing jams. (Some models won't serge when the cover is open.)

(B) *Keep cover closed while serging.*

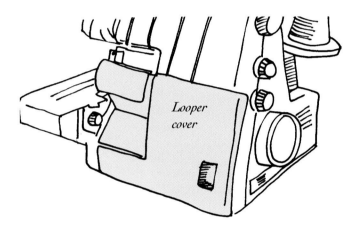

Looper cover

✧ Don't allow fabric trimmings or thread to fall into the looper area. (This can happen even when the looper cover is closed.)

✧ Examine both the upper and lower knife. Is the upper knife engaged for cutting? Is the lower knife aligned with the throat plate? If either knife is not properly positioned, the serger will not cut the fabric edge; the fabric will be wider than the stitch, causing jamming. Also, check the sharpness of the knives. See pages 32-33.

✧ Visually trace the threading path to check for hang-ups and improper paths (see pages 10, 14).

✧ Lengthen the stitch, particularly if using heavy or blended threads (C). The thicker threads take up more room, and if the stitch is too short, they will jam on the stitch finger (see pages 46-47).

(C) *Lengthen stitch for thick thread.*

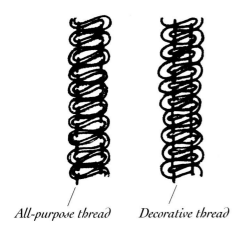

All-purpose thread   Decorative thread

✧ Change to the correct foot or plate. For instance, using the narrow finger for a wide stitch can cause jamming, as can using a wide finger for a narrow stitch.

✧ Use the correct needle position for the foot and/or throat plate. Some rolled-edge feet and throat plates are specifically designed to work with only the right needle position.

✧ Loosen looper thread tensions. If the tensions are too tight for the thread or fabric, jamming can result.

✧ Readjust for balanced tensions (see pages 8-9) throughout.

✧ On some models, avoid serging "on air." Instead, always lift the presser foot and insert fabric so the first stitch will be through fabric.

✧ Always place the thread chain under the foot and then pull it gently to advance the stitch (see page 10).

✧ Increase presser foot pressure. If it's too light for the fabric, the feed dogs may not be able to advance the fabric adequately.

✧ Compress fabric layers, or serge fewer layers. If too thick to fit into the "mouth" of the upper and lower knife, the serger won't cut and will probably jam. Also, when serging heavy or thick fabrics, the upper knife may need to be locked into position (consult your manual for this adjustment).

✧ Change to lighter weight or more tightly twisted threads. Some serger models are especially prone to jamming when using yarn.

✧ Clean the feed dogs, knives, and looper areas (see page 90).

✧ Replace or reposition the needle (see pages 28-29).

My Solutions:

Problem: Needle Insertion

Solutions:

◆ Consult the needle-replacement how-to's in your serger manual.

◆ Use the recommended needle size and type (either household or industrial) for your model (see page 84). Note the variety of industrial needle types (DCx1, BLx1, DBx1, JLx1); use the correct type for your model and the needle position.

◆ Before removing or inserting needles, turn the handwheel to raise the needle to its highest—and most accessible—position.

◆ To remove a needle, loosen the set-screw sufficiently. (Remember, turn right to tighten and left to loosen, or "righty-tighty, lefty-loosey.") Generally, less loosening is required for removing the needle than for inserting it.

Caution: Be careful not to unscrew a set-screw completely, risking losing the tiny but indispensable part. To prevent loss, magnetize your screwdriver tip by placing its tip on a magnetic pincushion (such as a Grabbit®); the set-screw will stick to the screwdriver even if totally loosened (A).

(A) *Magnetize screwdriver to hold set-screw. No more lost set-screws.*

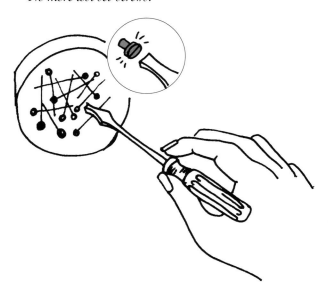

◆ If your serger has two or three set-screws, be sure you are loosening the correct one. Try loosening the other set-screw(s), too.

Note: If you have difficulty seeing or differentiating the needle slots, hold a small mirror—tiny, long-handled dental mirrors are perfect—under the needle clamp.

◆ If your serger has only one set-screw for both needles (B), remove both needles, loosen the set-screw further, then try reinserting both again.

(B) *Use tweezers for needle removal.*

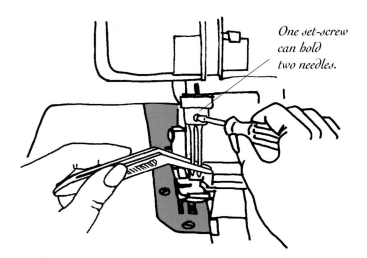

One set-screw can hold two needles.

◆ Get a good grip when holding and inserting needles. Use striated-tip tweezers, needle grippers, or small needlenose pliers.

◆ When inserting a needle, align it correctly. Household needles (flat-back shank) or industrial needles (usually round shank) should be inserted to align the groove in the front, and the scarf to the back (see page 84). The needle eye should face directly front (which can be a little tricky when inserting round-shank industrial needles).

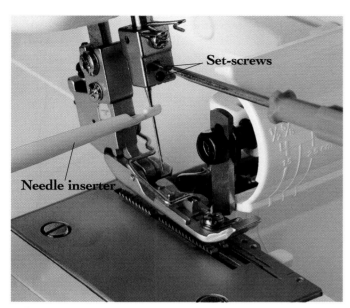

Shown above: *Insert any type or size serger needle completely and accurately by using a needle inserter.*

To align the needle accurately, try inserting the point of another needle into the eye; rotating it until the needle eye is parallel with the left edge of the throat plate; then tighten the set-screw (C). Or use a needle inserter (see photo above).

(C)

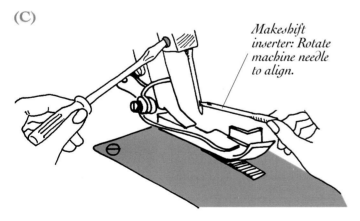

Makeshift inserter: Rotate machine needle to align.

◆ Push the needle all the way up into the slot. The set-screw may be blocking the slot; loosen as necessary. If it isn't inserted completely, the needle length and stitch timing will be out of sync, preventing stitch formation.

Note: Even when properly inserted, needles on multiple-needle sergers aren't necessarily level at the points. For instance, the left needle of a two-needle serger may be higher than the right needle.

◆ Loosen *all* set-screws if one won't loosen or tighten adequately. (Set-screws could be overtightened, causing an obstruction in the slot.)

◆ If after inserting a new needle, the serger fails to form a stitch, ask these questions:

✧ Was the correct needle type used?

✧ Was the needle placed in the correct needle slot for the foot or plate and the intended stitch?

✧ Was the needle inserted completely, and aligned accurately?

✧ Was the serger threaded properly?

My Solutions:

Problem: Needle Breakage

Solutions:

◆ Insert a new needle, correctly (see pages 28-29, 84). A wrong or improperly inserted needle can cause breakage.

◆ Change to a larger needle—your current needle size may be too delicate for your fabric and thread. Remember, however, most serger manufacturers do not recommend using a size larger than 14/90.

◆ Loosen the needle and upper looper tensions. Too-tight tension can bend, and actually break, a needle.

◆ Visually retrace threading paths to the needle. The thread could be wrapped around a guide or thread pin, or be caught in a spool notch.

◆ Don't tug on your fabric or the thread chain (A). This can cause needles to bend and hit the loopers.

(A)

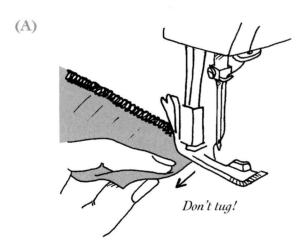

Don't tug!

◆ Check that you're using the correct foot and throat plate for the needle position. If the alignment is off, the needle can collide with the foot and/or throat plate.

◆ Avoid pulling or serging knots through the needle eyes. Although this is tempting when tying on threads to rethread, don't do it; the knots can bend or break the needles.

◆ Place pins perpendicular to the fabric edge, and remove before reaching the front of the presser foot (B). Use long, large-head pins, which are less likely to get lost in the nap of the fabric. Also, replace a needle after a run-in with a pin, even if it doesn't break (it will be dulled or damaged).

(B) *Remove pins before reaching foot.*

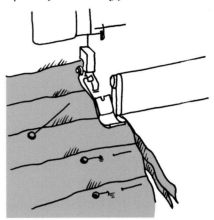

◆ Take care when serging over wire, fishing line, bead strands, or other heavy fillers, so the needle does not hit the filler. Try using a beading foot; the channels guide the filler precisely between the needle and the knives and within the stitch.

◆ Serge slowly on heavily textured fabrics (slubs, sequins, metallics), and use the largest needle possible (generally size 14/90).

◆ Even if you follow these precautions, keep a stock of needles on hand for more unexpected breakage.

My Solutions:

Problem: Runs or Holes in Fabric

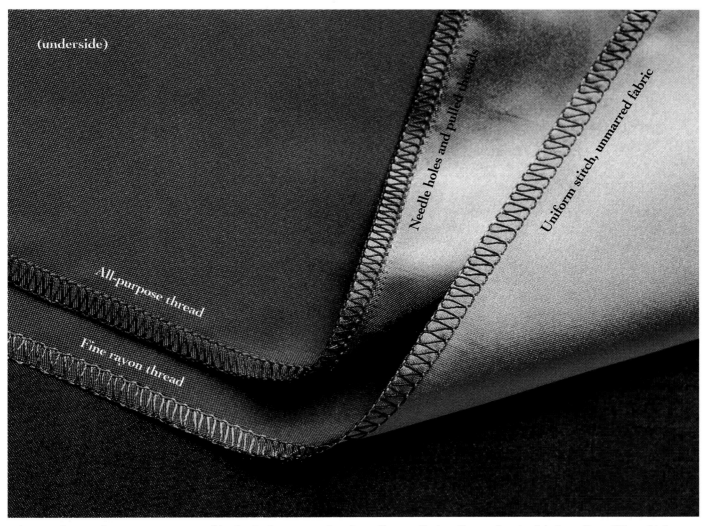

(underside)

Needle holes and pulled threads

Uniform stitch, unmarred fabric

All-purpose thread

Fine rayon thread

Shown above: *Changing to a new needle that's the correct size (usually smaller) and type for the fabric, and avoiding thick or wiry thread in the needle will correct/prevent most problems with pulled threads, runs, and holes along the needleline.*

Solutions:

◆ Replace the needle. The one currently being used is probably blunt, creating pulled threads, runs, or holes.

◆ Change to a smaller needle, a ballpoint needle (industrial and household types), or stretch needle (household). See page 84.

◆ Lengthen the stitch. Needle holes too close together can weaken the edge of loosely woven or unstable fabrics. In some cases, the stitch can actually be pulled off the fabric edge.

◆ Use a finer or softer thread. Thick or wiry threads can cause holes along serged needleline.

◆ Loosen the needle tension slightly.

◆ To prevent runs when finishing cross-grain edges of ribbing or interlock knits: Fold a ⅜" allowance to the wrong side, then serge along the fold without trimming or stretching.

My Solutions:

Problem: Ragged or Uncut Edges

Solutions:

◆ Engage the upper knife so that it's in the cutting position (A). On some models this is a rotating mechanism; on others, you dial to move the upper knife. If unsure how to move and position the upper knife, consult your manual. If you have moved the upper knife into the cutting position, but it still does not cut, consult your dealer.

(A) *Two knife styles in cutting positions:*

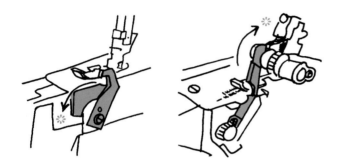

❊ *Disengaged (no cutting) positions*

Note: On some older (but very popular) models, the upper knife cannot be adjusted to a noncutting position. If your serger has this style knife system, and you suspect the upper knife is out of position for cutting, see your dealer.

◆ Move the fabric to the right to allow for trimming, which will neaten a ragged raw edge.

◆ Move the fabric to the left to trim less. Or pretrim the fabric edge. Too much fabric to the right of the knives can jam the cutting mechanism.

◆ Reset the lower knife blade (it might have been incorrectly positioned or slipped out of alignment). This adjustment involves moving the lower knife back into alignment with the throat plate: Loosen the screw, realign the lower knife blade, and finally, tighten the screw to prevent further slippage (B).

(B) *Two lower blade styles in cutting positions:*

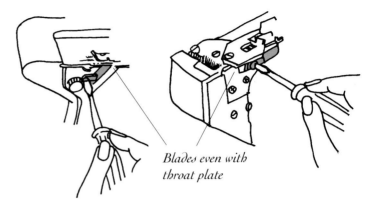

Blades even with throat plate

◆ Determine if the fabric layers are too thick to enter the knife "mouth," and hence, be cut. (The mouth is open widest when the needle is in its highest position.) If necessary, compress the layers with conventional zigzagging, or decrease the number of layers. Or pretrim the entire allowance, eliminating the need to cut while serging (C).

(C)

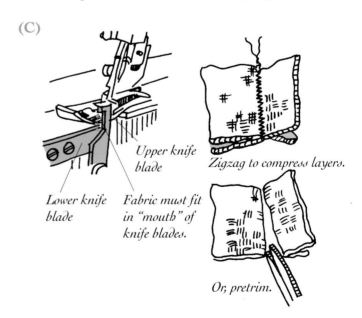

Upper knife blade

Zigzag to compress layers.

Lower knife blade

Fabric must fit in "mouth" of knife blades.

Or, pretrim.

◆ Lock the upper knife blade (D, page 33) if serging heavy fabrics. (This feature is not available on all sergers—check your manual.) Or tighten the upper knife blade screw to ensure steady alignment while cutting.

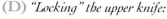
(D) *"Locking" the upper knife:*

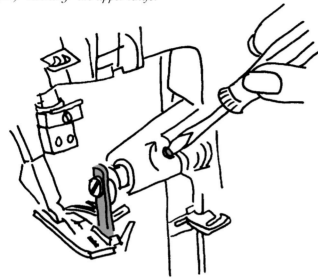

◆ Clean lint and threads—both of which can hamper cutting—between the upper and lower knife blades.

◆ Lubricate the blades regularly (see page 90).

◆ Look for nicks and worn shiny spots on the upper and lower knife blades **(E)**. Serging over pins is the primary cause of nicks, and worn spots will be more prevalent if you serge on heavy synthetics (such as nylon outerwear, Lycra®-blend knits, and polar fleece).

(E) *Lower knife blades*

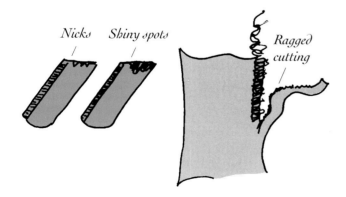

Nicks   *Shiny spots*   *Ragged cutting*

◆ Replace the lower, stationary knife blade—it's the most likely to be dull. Remove the dull blade by unscrewing the screw. Long (10" or longer) screwdrivers provide the best leverage for loosening and tightening. Slip the replacement blade in place and retighten the screw.

Note: Active or professional serger-seamsters may need to change the lower blade two or three times a year, while infrequent users may change it only every other year. A replacement blade is generally part of a serger's standard accessory kit, but it's smart to keep another spare on hand.

◆ Investigate replacing the upper, movable knife blade, which is made of a tougher carbide composite. The upper blade may never need to be replaced. But if it looks worn or nicked, or if changing the lower blade doesn't improve cutting quality, the upper blade may need to be changed, too.

Note: Call your dealer for replacements and installation estimates. Upper knives are not usually standard accessories and can cost up to four times more than lower blades. Professional installation is recommended, because alignment with the lower knife blade is so crucial to the correct cutting action. Also, inquire about upper knife blade resharpening services.

My Solutions:

Problem: Puckers

Puckers

Loosened needle thread

Shortened stitch

Minus differential feed

Stabilized edge

(top side)

Shown above: *Puckering is reduced by loosening the needle thread tension, shortening the stitch length, adjusting for minus differential feed, and/or stabilizing the edge.* **Note:** *All samples are in progress, from puckered (left) to flat (right).*

Solutions:

◆ Loosen the needle tension slightly, then test-serge. Repeat until the puckers flatten (A, page 35). The needle tension is the most likely to cause puckering because it controls the stitch feed and length. If loosening the needle tension doesn't correct the puckering, try loosening the looper tensions slightly.

◆ Visually trace threading paths, looking for tangled or trapped thread—particularly the needle thread. Check for thread catching on or wrapping around the spools or cones, thread pins, telescopic thread guide, tension guides and controls, needle-clamp guides, and needles.

(A)

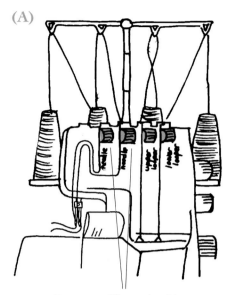

Loosen needle tension(s).

◆ Shorten the stitch length. The less fabric between each stitch, the less puckering.

◆ If your machine features differential feeding, adjust to a minus-setting (below 1) (B). The minus-setting changes how the fabric feeds: Less fabric is taken in under the foot than is released out the back (see pages 38, 69). Combine with taut-serging (see right) if puckering persists.

◆ Taut-serge: Hold the fabric flat and taut, in front of and behind the foot (C). Be careful not to pull too rigorously, which can cause the needle to bend or break.

C) Puckers minimized: Taut-serge.

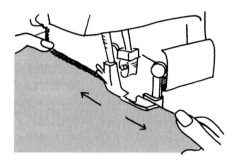

◆ Replace a blunt, burred, or bent needle.

◆ Use a finer thread and smaller needle.

◆ Change to a more stable thread in the needle. Monofilament-nylon and woolly stretch nylon, for example, stretch as they travel through the thread path, tightening tensions.

◆ Adjust for heavier presser foot pressure when serging lightweight fabrics.

◆ Stabilize the edge or seam with another layer of fabric, fusible interfacing, or lightweight trim. The stabilized fabric will be flatter between each stitch.

Or serge over a strip of water-soluble stabilizer, which will stabilize and smooth the edge, minimizing puckering. The stabilizer will dissolve during the first laundering.

◆ Do not prewash your fabric. Finishes discourage puckering.

◆ Watch for label glue on the spool or cone, which will stop or slow down the thread feed and can cause puckers. Scratch or wind it off, or dissolve the glue with rubbing alcohol.

My Solutions:

(B) *Three differential feed adjustment styles:*

Below "1" controls puckering.

Problem: Excessive Stretching

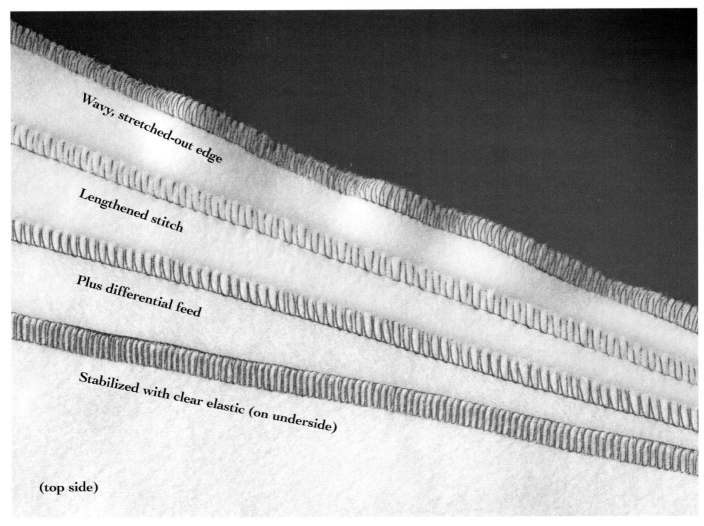

Wavy, stretched-out edge

Lengthened stitch

Plus differential feed

Stabilized with clear elastic (on underside)

(top side)

Shown above: *Control unwanted stretching by lengthening the stitch, adjusting for a plus differential feed setting, and/or stabilizing the edge by serging over clear elastic.*

Solutions:

◆ Lengthen the stitch. The more fabric between each stitch, the less stretching.

◆ Trim at least ¼" while serging **(A, page 37)**. Less stretching will occur when the foot is on the more stable area of the fabric—in from the edge.

◆ If your machine features differential feeding, readjust to a plus-setting (above 1). The plus-setting changes how the fabric feeds; more fabric is taken in under the foot than is released out the back (see pages 38, 69). If excessive stretching persists, combine with ease-plusing (see page 37).

(A) *For less stretching, trim edge.*

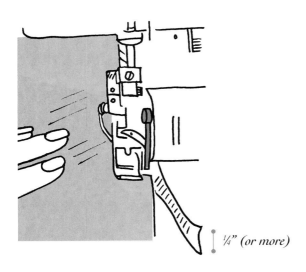

¼" *(or more)*

(B) *Ease-plusing minimizes stretching.*

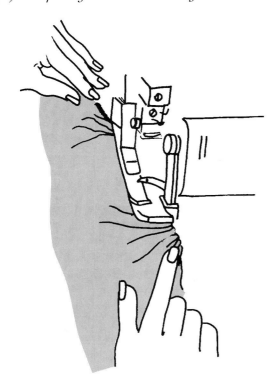

◆ Ease-plus: While serging, push the fabric under the foot while holding your finger behind the foot, slowing the release **(B)**.

◆ Adjust for lighter presser foot pressure (see page 70).

◆ Don't stretch the edge while serging, or allow the fabric to hang off your serging table. If you serge over a stretched edge, the stitches will hold the stretched position.

◆ Use a finer thread. Heavy decorative thread, in particular, has a tendency to stretch the edge.

◆ Serge over (not through) filler such as ⅛" cording or elastic. After serging, draw up to the desired size.

◆ Serge through ¼"- to ½"-wide clear elastic, placed on the underside of the edge. Pull the elastic slightly while serging to draw up the edge and prevent stretching (see photo on page 36).

◆ Before serging, stabilize the edge or seam with another layer of fabric or fusible interfacing. The stabilized fabric will stretch less.

◆ Fold under ⅜" to the wrong side and serge over, but don't trim, the foldline.

◆ Serge along the lengthwise, or another more stable grainline.

◆ Don't prewash fabric. Finishes discourage stretching.

My Solutions:

Problem: Differential Feed Isn't Working

Solutions:

To enhance easing or gathering:

◆ Make sure the feed is adjusted to a plus-setting. The higher the number, the more gathering.

◆ Lengthen the stitch to allow for more easing or gathering under the stitch.

◆ Tighten needle tension. And make sure the threads are fully engaged in the tension controls.

◆ Ease-plus to enhance "plus" differential feeding (see page 37).

◆ Use a lighter, or softer fabric, or serge only one layer.

To control stretching (see also pages 36-37):

◆ Make sure the feed is adjusted to a plus-setting. The higher the number, the more it draws up the fabric.

◆ Lengthen the stitch to allow for more easing under the stitch.

◆ Ease-plus (see page 37) to enhance a plus-setting.

◆ Decrease presser foot pressure (see page 70).

◆ Tighten needle tension and check that threads are fully engaged in tension controls.

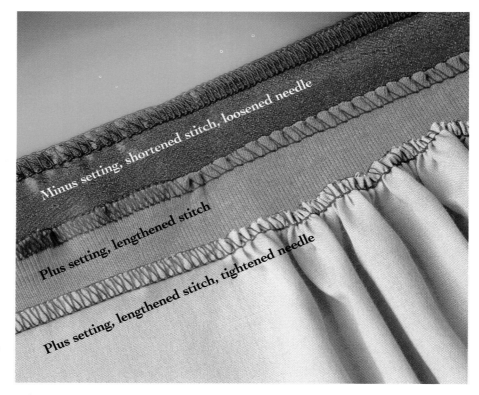

Minus setting, shortened stitch, loosened needle

Plus setting, lengthened stitch

Plus setting, lengthened stitch, tightened needle

To control puckering (see also pages 34-35):

◆ Make sure the feed is adjusted to a minus-setting (below 1). The lower the number, the less puckering.

◆ Shorten the stitch. The less fabric between each stitch, the less puckering.

◆ Loosen needle tension.

◆ Taut-serge (see page 35) to enhance a minus-setting.

◆ Decrease presser foot pressure (see page 70).

My Solutions:

Problem: Seam Spreads or Unravels

overlock. Or, if available, change to a stitch that incorporates chainstitching (see pages 66-67).

◆ Avoid bulk at seam intersections. Alternate allowance directions. Also reinforce strained seams by straight stitching over the serged seamline at the intersection (A).

To prevent seams or edges from unraveling:

◆ Use seam sealant to seal the beginning and end of a serged seam or edge. Dab on the stitches, let dry, trim tails.

◆ Bury the chain tail within the stitch (see page 68).

◆ Secure seam ends with serging (B). At the beginning of a seam, serge over the chain tail. At the end of a seam, serge directly over the last few stitches.

My Solutions:

Solutions:

To lessen seam-spread:

Note: All serged seams (with the exception of the chainstitch) will spread more than a conventional straight stitch. Also, seams in spongy knits will spread less than those in flat-surfaced wovens.

◆ Tighten needle tension and make sure the needle thread is fully engaged in the tension control. Loosening of the looper tensions may also be required.

◆ Use a stretchy thread, such as monofilament-nylon or woolly stretch nylon in the needle position.

◆ Change stitches. For instance, change from a 2-thread wrapped/seam to a 3-thread

(A) Alternate seam allowance directions.

Reinforce with straight stitching.

(B) Securing seam ends:

Beginning: Serge over chain.   *End: Pull threads off stitch finger, flip fabric over, and serge.*

Problem: Can't Determine a Seam Edge

Solutions:

◆ If not already marked, mark the needleline positions (seamlines) on the top of the foot **(A)**. Remember, knives cut about ½" of fabric before forming the stitch. It's important to watch the foot rather than the needle, thus preventing regrettable trimming errors.

(A)

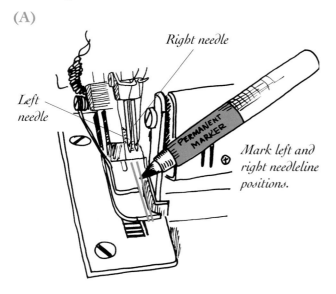

Right needle

Left needle

PERMANENT MARKER

Mark left and right needleline positions.

◆ If not already labeled, mark standard ⅝" seam allowance lines on the looper cover (on tape, if you prefer). Or purchase special adhesive seamline guides **(B)**. There will be a different seamline marking for each needle position.

(B) *On looper cover, use decal or mark seamlines.*

Adhesive seam guide

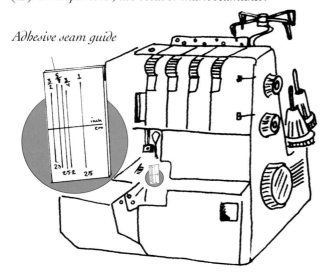

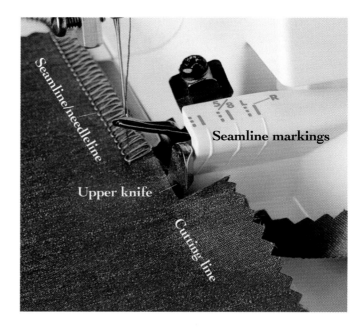

Seamline/needleline

Seamline markings

Upper knife

Cutting line

◆ Serge on scraps to determine the correct seam width, and practice uniform trimming. The actual serged seam allowance width is the distance from the leftmost needle to the knife.

◆ Don't miscalculate seam allowance widths when serge-finishing:

◇ If you serge-finish before conventional straight-stitch seaming, barely skim the edges to maintain the intended allowance width.

◇ If you serge finish after conventional straight-stitch seaming, consider cutting wider seam allowances (up to 1"). The edges will be trimmable (up to ¼"), easier to handle, press flat, and less prone to trimming accidents.

My Solutions:

Problem: Ugly Curves and Corners

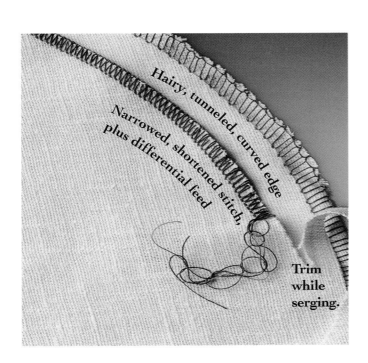

Hairy, tunneled, curved edge

Narrowed, shortened stitch, plus differential feed

Trim while serging.

◆ If tunneling (bunching of the fabric under the stitch) occurs, narrow the stitch slightly.

◆ Adjust differential feed to a plus-setting when serging the most stretch-prone section of the curve.

◆ For improved coverage and uniformity on outside corners, shorten the stitch length.

◆ Trim while serging to neaten and discourage stretching.

Outside Corners:

◆ Serge off the fabric edge, turn the fabric, then serge the adjacent edge **(B)**. Slightly rounded corners, as shown, look more square. Finish by dabbing with seam sealant; allow to dry and trim the chain tail. Or bury the tail (see page 68).

(B)

Too pointed   *Slightly rounded corners look more square:*

Needleline   *Needleline*

Trim ⅟₁₆"–⅛" more at corner areas, tapering to normal needleline.

My Solutions:

Solutions:

Curves:

◆ Practice on scraps, watching the knife rather than the needle, and using both hands to guide the fabric. (You will improve.)

◆ Serge slowly and consistently. For outside curves, move the fabric to the right, forming a straight line in front of the presser foot. For inside curves, move the fabric to the left, forming a straight line in front of the presser foot **(A)**.

(A)

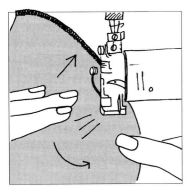

Outside curve

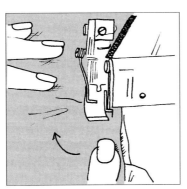

Inside curve

Problem: Rolled-Edge Snafus

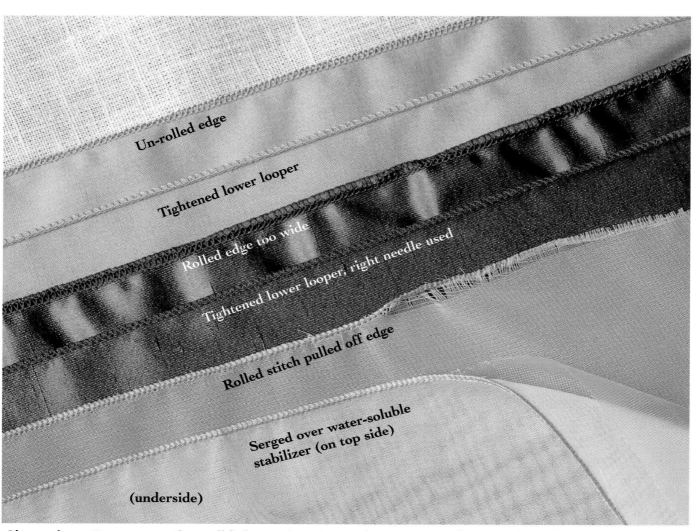

Un-rolled edge

Tightened lower looper

Rolled edge too wide

Tightened lower looper, right needle used

Rolled stitch pulled off edge

Serged over water-soluble stabilizer (on top side)

(underside)

Shown above: *For narrow, uniform rolled edges, tighten the lower looper, fine-tune the stitch width, and if necessary, strengthen the edge with water-soluble stabilizer.* ***Note:*** *All samples are shown from the underside.*

Solutions:

To encourage the edge to roll:

◆ Properly adjust tensions for a narrow rolled edge.

✧ 3-thread: Tighten the lower looper (probably completely) and loosen the upper looper so that the fabric rolls and the thread wraps the edge. The needle tension may also require some tightening.

✧ 2-thread: Tighten the needle (probably completely) and loosen the looper so the fabric rolls and the thread wraps the edge.

Note: Enhance tightening of the lower looper thread (of a 3-thread stitch) or the needle thread (of a 2-thread stitch) by using stretchy thread. Woolly stretch nylon or monofilament-nylon threads stretch as they pass through guides, tightening the tensions beyond adjusted settings.

◆ Widen the stitch width or bite (see page 73). More fabric will be rolled inside the stitch.

Or use the left needle position. Refer to your machine manual or consult with your dealer to see if this is possible and safe with your serger. If still uncertain, insert the needle in the left position and slowly turn the handwheel, making sure the stitch advances and the needle doesn't hit the foot or throat plate.

◆ Be certain you're using the narrow stitch finger. On some machines this change is dialed; on others narrowing the stitch finger requires changing the foot and/or throat plate (A).

(A) Stitch finger types:

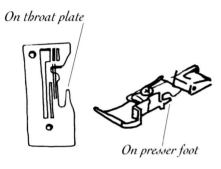

On throat plate

On presser foot

◆ Shorten the stitch.

◆ If the fabric is too heavy or stiff to roll, change to a wrapped stitch, for a similar look (B).

◆ Change to a softer, lighter-weight fabric that will roll more readily around the stitch finger.

To make the stitch narrow enough (see also pages 22-23):

◆ Narrow the stitch width/bite.

◆ Use the correct (usually right) needle position.

◆ Change to the correct foot or throat plate.

◆ Tighten the looper tensions.

◆ Use finer thread in the loopers.

◆ Use a softer and/or thinner fabric. Or prewash your fabric to soften the finish.

To prevent the stitch from pulling off the edge:

◆ Widen the stitch or bite.

◆ Lengthen the stitch slightly, which will make fewer needle holes in the fabric.

◆ Use a smaller, sharper needle, which will make smaller needle holes in the fabric.

◆ Turn under ¼" allowance and serge along the folded edge without trimming.

◆ Serge over a strip of water-soluble stabilizer, placed over fabric edge (see photo on page 42).

◆ Serge along a stronger, more stable grainline.

◆ Change your fabric or method of edge finishing.

My Solutions:

(B)

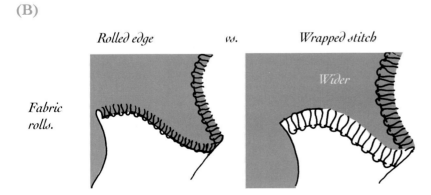

Rolled edge   *vs.*   *Wrapped stitch*

Wider

Fabric rolls.

Similar effects (both showcase upper looper thread), except wrapped stitch is wider, and no fabric is rolled within it.

Problem: Faulty Flatlocking

Shown above: *Easy tension adjustments and allowing looper thread loops to hang over the fabric edge or fold while serging are the keys to flat and stable flatlocking.*

Solutions:

Note: Familiarize yourself with flatlocking loops and ladders (see pages 45, 66-67).

◆ Properly adjust tensions for flatlocking:

◇ 3-thread: Loosen the needle tension almost completely, tighten the lower looper tension almost completely, and, if necessary, loosen the upper looper tension slightly (A, page 45). If tightening beyond tension settings is required, use woolly stretch nylon or lightweight mono-filament-nylon thread in the lower looper.

◇ 2-thread: Loosen the looper tension slightly, especially if using heavier, decorative thread. Loosen the needle tension slightly if flatlocking thick fabrics (B, page 45).

Note: Minimal adjustments are required because a balanced 2-thread stitch is a true flatlock. See page 8.

(A) *3-thread flatlock:*

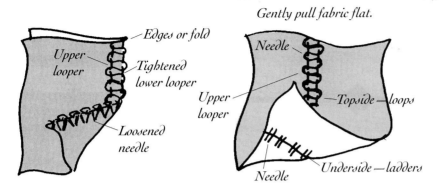

(B) *2-thread flatlock (needle and looper threads balanced):*

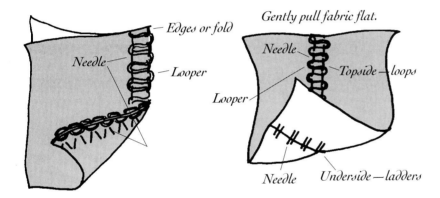

Also, visually trace threading paths, checking for hang-ups; tighten the looper or upper looper slightly; and/or lengthen the stitch.

◆ To correct hairy edges or unraveling edges, shorten the stitch, or use heavier thread in the looper or upper looper (see pages 16-17).

Or serge-finish the edges before flatlocking them, using fine, matching thread and a narrow, long stitch.

Or press under the seam allowances, and flatlock the seamline folds together.

Note: Flatlocking is nearly mistake-proof on spongy, ravel-free sweatshirt and interlock knits.

My Solutions:

◆ Achieve super-flat flatlocking by allowing the stitches to hang off the fold or edge while serging.

◆ Use the correct threads in the proper locations for decorative flatlocking:

◇ When loops will be exposed, use heavier, decorative thread, or blended threads in the upper looper of a 3-thread flatlock, and in the looper of a 2-thread flatlock.

◇ When ladders will be exposed, use topstitching thread or buttonhole twist in the needle of a 2- or 3-thread flatlock. The needle thread must be fine enough to pass through the needle eye, slip into the front needle groove, and penetrate the fabric.

◇ Use serger or all-purpose thread in the lower looper of a 3-thread flatlock (only a fine line of thread shows on the loop side of the stitch)

◆ To correct irregular loops on a flatlock stitch, serge an even width from the fold, or trim the fabric while serging.

Problem: Decorative Thread Confusion

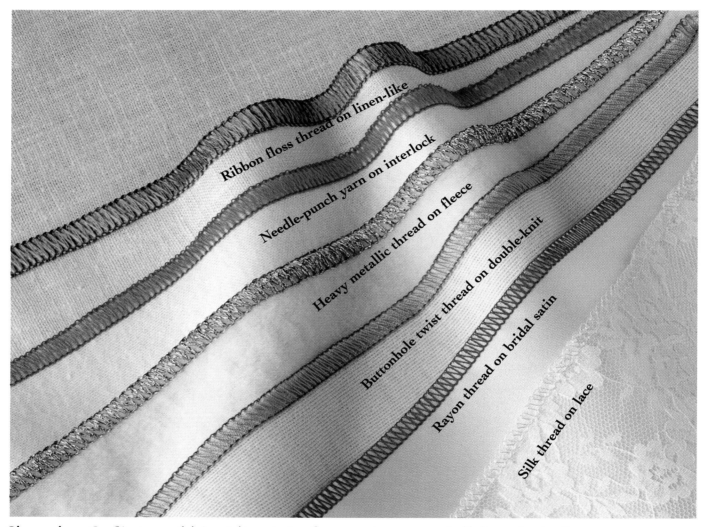

Ribbon floss thread on linen-like

Needle-punch yarn on interlock

Heavy metallic thread on fleece

Buttonhole twist thread on double-knit

Rayon thread on bridal satin

Silk thread on lace

Shown above: *Coordinate your fabric weight, content, and care requirements to suitable decorative threads.*

Solutions:

◆ Master threading decorative threads. Use tweezers to pull limp strands through the guides. The eyes can be threaded with a thread cradle, looper threader (see page 75), needle threader, or floss threader (A, page 47). Pull fine, limp threads through by tying on to a strand of all-purpose thread.

◆ Start with smoother, tightly twisted decorative threads. Then graduate to heavier types. Buttonhole twist (or topstitching thread) is easy to handle and is available in every shade imaginable.

Note: To test the suitability of heavy threads, pull two strands through the upper looper eye (see right for threading options); if they pass through easily, the thread, yarn, or ribbon is thin enough for serging.

(A) Threading made easy:

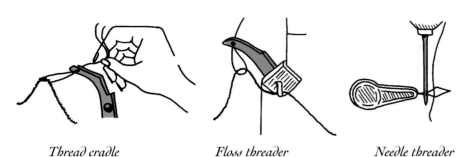

Thread cradle   Floss threader   Needle threader

◆ Test-serge. Experiment with stitch length (2mm or longer for heavy threads), width, tension, and differential feed settings, test-serging on long strips of the actual project fabric.

◆ Coordinate your fabric to suitable decorative threads:

✧ Cottons (light- to mid-weight): woolly stretch nylon, buttonhole twist (or topstitching thread), metallic, rayon.

✧ Cottons and cotton blends (decorator weight): all decorative thread types (use heavier weights on heavier fabrics).

✧ Interlock and jersey knits: all decorative thread types, except woven ribbon.

✧ Sweatshirtings and polar fleece: woolly stretch nylon, buttonhole twist, pearl cotton, crochet thread, heavy metallic thread/yarn, heavy rayon, ribbon floss, yarn.

✧ Lycra®-blend knits: woolly stretch nylon, some metallic and heavy metallic.

✧ Sweaterknits: woolly stretch nylon, buttonhole twist, pearl cotton, crochet thread, heavy metallic, heavy rayon, ribbon/ribbon floss, silk (heavy), yarn.

✧ Lace (lightweight), tulle and netting: woolly stretch nylon, metallic, rayon, silk.

✧ Silk-likes, silks, satins: woolly stretch nylon, button-hole twist (or topstitching thread), metallic, heavy metallic, rayon, heavy rayon, silk.

✧ Wool, silk, cotton suitings: buttonhole twist (or top-stitching thread), pearl cotton, crochet thread, heavy metallic, heavy rayon, silk (heavy), yarn.

◆ Coordinate the thread and the stitch. Refer to the "Thread Chart" on pages 86-87. Decorative thread is most suited—but not limited to—where it can be watched easily while serging (such as the upper looper) and is exposed in most serged stitches.

◆ Buy enough decorative thread for your entire project, including test-serging. For each exposed looper, multiply the length of the edge to be serged by 10; add one more spool or cone to that total. Our don't-run-out rule for decorative-serging projects: 400 to 500 yards for each exposed looper, and 250 yards for each needle or tightened-down looper.

◆ Match care and wear compatibilities. If the project will be laundered, use a washable, colorfast thread. If the serged stitches will be subject to abrasion, use highly twisted cotton or nylon threads (rayon threads, in general, do not wear as well).

◆ Blend different decorative, all-purpose and/or serger threads to increase the coverage, or to mix shades and textures. Place the additional spools or cones on the empty thread pins or a Thread Palette (see page 76).

My Solutions:

Problem: Irregular or No Decorative Stitch

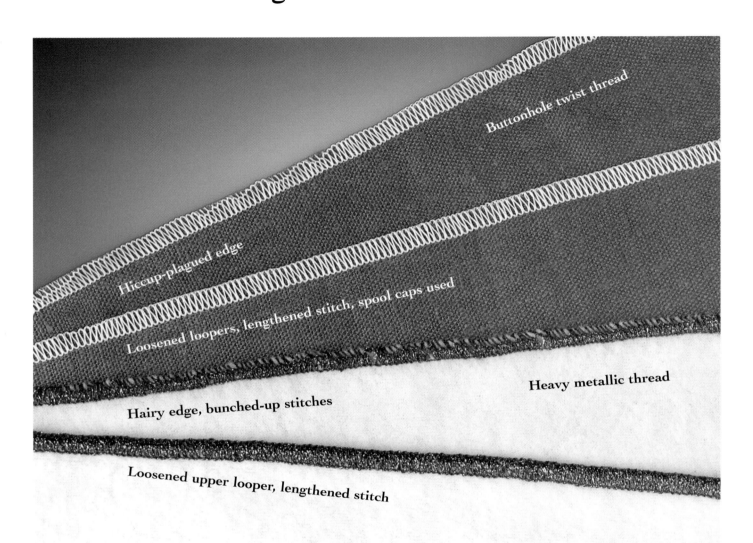

Buttonhole twist thread

Hiccup-plagued edge

Loosened loopers, lengthened stitch, spool caps used

Hairy edge, bunched-up stitches

Heavy metallic thread

Loosened upper looper, lengthened stitch

Shown above: Decorative stitch irregularities, such as hiccups and hairy edges, can often be solved by loosening the looper thread tensions, slightly lengthening the stitch, and/or using spool caps or thread nets (depending on thread type).

Solutions:

Note: Also refer to pages 10, 11, 14-15, 26-27.

To facilitate stitch formation:

◆ Visually trace the threading paths. Confirm that the needle and loopers are threaded, and that none of the tension controls or guides have been missed.

◆ Be sure you're using the correct type and size needle, and

it's positioned properly. If you're using decorative thread in the needle, move up to a size 14/90 (a larger-eyed) needle.

◆ Lower the presser foot. Some sergers won't form a stitch with the foot up.

◆ When starting to serge, place all the threads above the throat plate and under the foot. Gently pull on the thread tails while advancing the stitch (see page 10).

◆ Loosen the looper tensions.

◆ Change threads. Too-stiff thread won't loop enough to catch the needle thread and form the stitch.

To prevent thread breakage:

◆ Check the threading paths, making sure thread isn't caught on any of the guides, or wrapped around a thread pin, looper, or the needle.

◆ Lengthen the stitch to accommodate thicker thread.

◆ Loosen the upper looper tension. For some heavy threads, ribbons, and yarns, you may need to remove the strand completely from the tension disc or dial (A).

To correct irregular stitches:

◆ Visually trace the threading paths, checking for thread wrapped around guides, caught on thread pins, etc.

◆ Serge an even width from the fold, or trim the fabric while stitching (see page 37).

◆ Facilitate smooth, even thread feeding by using thread nets for cones (especially for rayon threads), caps for spools (see page 19), Horizontal Thread Holders for narrow tubes, and spool rings for cones, spools, and tubes (see pages 74, 76).

◆ Lengthen the stitch slightly. This will tighten the looper tensions and often smooth out the stitch.

◆ Tighten the tensions slightly: first the loopers, then, if necessary, the needle.

My Solutions:

(A) For extra-loose tensions: Remove thread from tension control.

Tape over lay-in path, or skip tension dial.

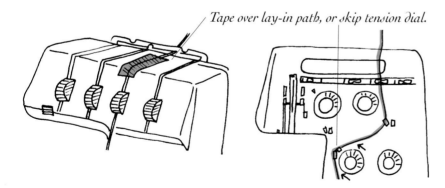

◆ Rethread, following the correct sequence for your serger. Bring all threads above the throat plate before beginning to serge.

◆ Change threads. The one you are using may be too stiff, thick, or nubby.

Quick Fixes

Problem: Serger Runs Slowly, or Not At All
Solutions:

◆ Check wall, power, and/or foot control connections. Also, make sure the looper cover is closed.

◆ Gain full use of foot control: Prevent movement during use, and look for obstructions under pedal.

◆ Change to faster stitch-speed setting (if possible).

◆ Disengage, then re-engage, the knives.

◆ Use a lighter-weight, less-bulky fabric.

◆ Clean and oil the serger (see page 90).

Problem: Can't Thread Lower Looper Easily
Solutions:

◆ If available, use the self-threading feature.

◆ Make sure the looper cover and all casing doors are open for easy access to the lower looper.

◆ Turn the handwheel to move the lower looper into the most accessible position.

◆ Use a looper threader (A).

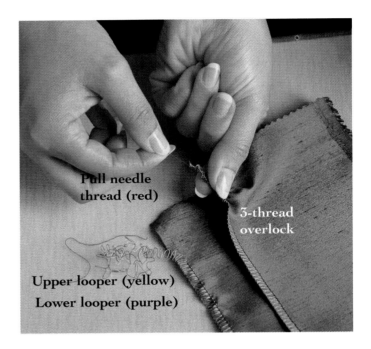

Pull needle thread (red)

3-thread overlock

Upper looper (yellow)
Lower looper (purple)

Problem: Can't Remove Serged Stitches Quickly
Solutions:

◆ Pull threads, rather than ripping out, as follows:

✧ On a 2-thread overedge or flatlock: Pull the needle and looper threads simultaneously.

✧ On a 2-thread chainstitch: Pull the looper thread away from the thicker, looped end of the stitch. (Might may be difficult to see: If the looper thread isn't releasing, pull from the other direction.)

✧ On a 3- or 3/4-thread overlock: Pull the shortest thread—the needle thread; the looper threads will "fall" off (see photo above).

✧ On a 3-thread flatlock: Pull the shortest thread—the lower looper; the needle and upper looper threads will "fall" off.

✧ On rolled or wrapped edges: If possible, simply trim the edge off, close to the needleline.

◆ Rip, rather than pull out threads: Slip a seam ripper under either the upper or lower looper

(A) *Streamline threading:*

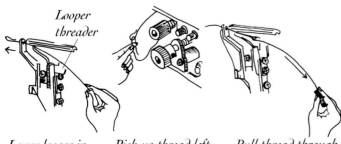

Looper threader

Lower looper in far right position.　*Pick up thread left of lower looper.*　*Pull thread through eye or guide.*

Quick Fixes

threads. Pick off the clipped threads (for easy removal, try an adhesive lint roller).

Problem: Running Out of Looper Thread
Solutions:

◆ Use larger spools or cones for loopers. The upper looper of a 3-thread and the looper of a 2-thread will consume the most thread for flatlocking, rolled edging, and wrapped stitching (see pages 66-67).

◆ If using low-yardage spools rather than cones, buy twice as many for the loopers as you do the needle positions. Or buy higher-yield cones for the loopers, and lower-yield spools for the needles.

Problem: Can't Serge Over Bulky Seams
Solutions:

◆ Place a cardboard or credit card shim under the presser foot (slightly left of the needleline), before and after the seam (B).

(B) *Serge over bulky seams:*

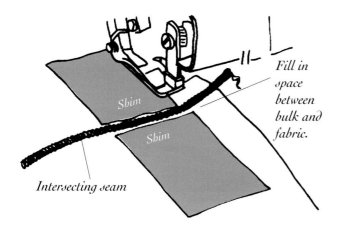

Fill in space between bulk and fabric.

Shim

Shim

Intersecting seam

◆ Minimize bulk by alternating intersecting seam allowance directions (see page 39).

Problem: Constant Tension Adjustments
Solutions:

◆ Check threading paths, making sure the threads are fully engaged in the tension controls.

◆ Understand that tensions usually need adjustments when changing thread types and weights; fabric types, weights, and layers; stitch width and length; differential feed.

◆ If tensions continually demand adjusting, even while all other factors remain constant—thread, fabric, stitch width and length, differential feed—consult your dealer.

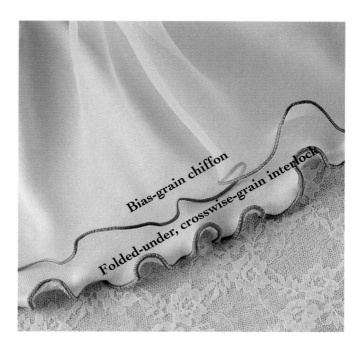

Bias-grain chiffon

Folded-under, crosswise-grain interlock

Problem: Edge Won't "Lettuce"
Solutions:

◆ Start with a fabric that stretches: the crosswise grain of interlock, rib, or Lycra®-blend knits; crosswise grain of polar fleece; or bias grain of wovens.

◆ Adjust differential feed to the lowest minus-setting (see pages 38, 69).

◆ Taut-serge: Stretch the fabric in front of and behind the presser foot while serging (see page 35).

◆ Shorten the stitch length.

Quick Fixes

Problem: Seams Pop in Stretch Fabric

Solutions:

◆ Stretch the seam slightly while serging. For the most stretch, use a 3-thread overlock.

◆ Loosen needle tension(s) slightly.

◆ Use woolly stretch nylon in the needle (will require additional needle-tension loosening).

◆ Use polyester or polyester-blend thread rather than 100% cotton, in the needle.

Problem: Thread Shreds During Serging

Solutions:

◆ Use high-quality thread.

◆ Replace the needle. It may be dull or damaged.

◆ Use a needle one size larger. Or use a topstitching or specialty needle, such as Schmetz Embroidery or Metalfil (see page 84).

◆ Blend shred-prone thread with a strong thread, such as woolly stretch nylon (see page 86).

Problem: Tinsel Metallic Thread Twists, Breaks

Solutions:

◆ Use a Horizontal Thread Holder so the thread can feed consistently twist-free (see page 74).

◆ Before serging again, rethread, completely straightening the strand.

Problem: Stitches Bunch Up On Elastic

Solutions:

◆ Adjust for the longest stitch length.

◆ Allow an extra 2" to 3" of elastic. Stitch into this extension before placing the fabric under the elastic, then anchor the two layers together with a few stitches. While stretching the elastic in front of the foot, pull on the elastic behind the foot to advance the stitch and maintain an even feed (C). (Also see "Elastic Foot," page 82.)

(C) *Smooth-serging elastic:*

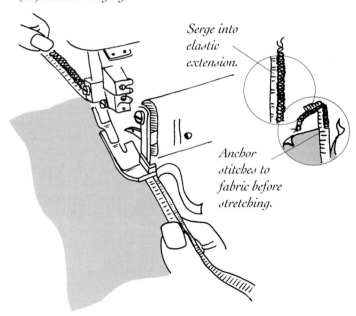

Serge into elastic extension.

Anchor stitches to fabric before stretching.

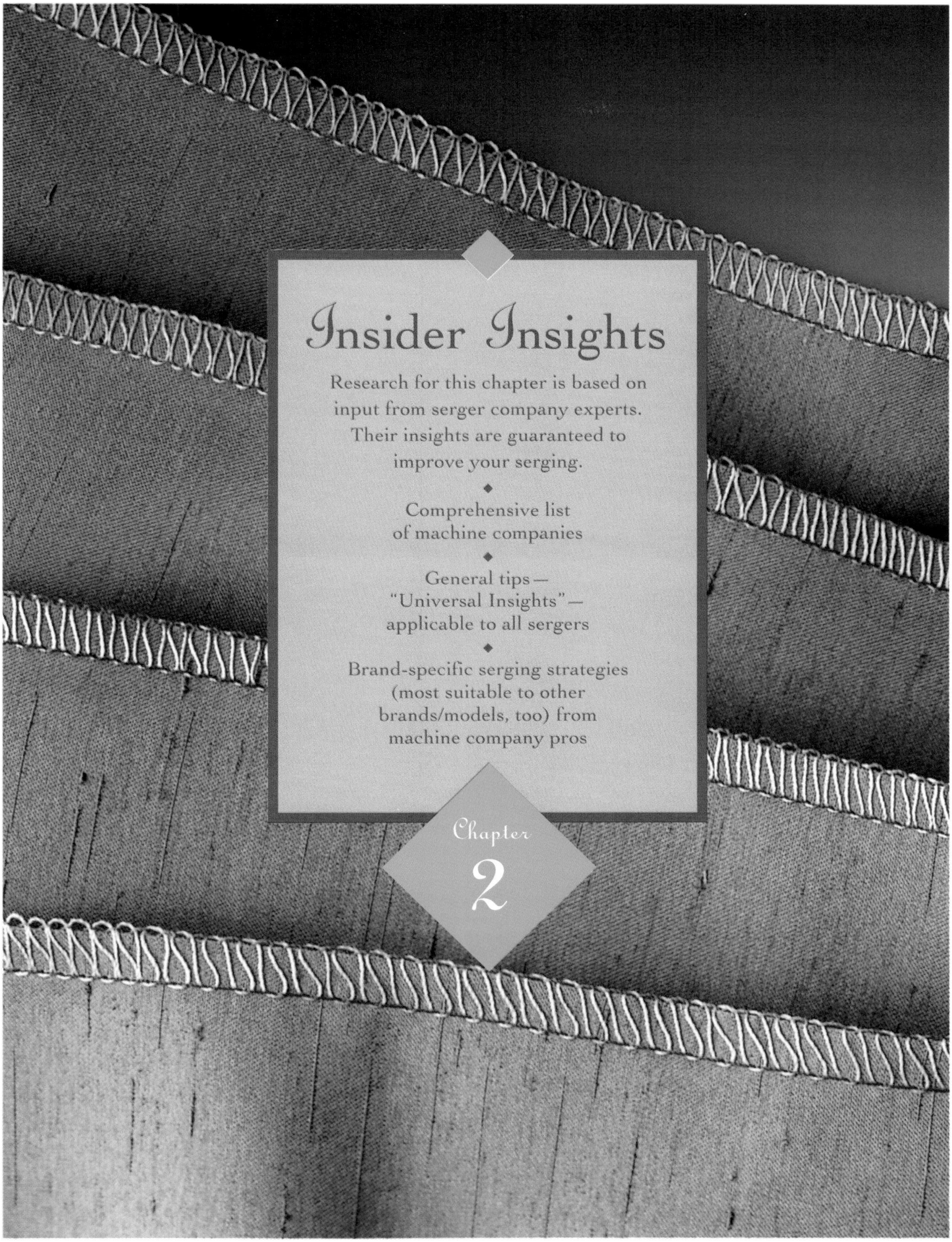

Insider Insights

Research for this chapter is based on input from serger company experts. Their insights are guaranteed to improve your serging.

◆

Comprehensive list of machine companies

◆

General tips— "Universal Insights"— applicable to all sergers

◆

Brand-specific serging strategies (most suitable to other brands/models, too) from machine company pros

Chapter

2

Universal Insights

After interviewing our many serger company contacts, we discovered some tips to be universal to all brands and models:

◆ Check threading paths carefully.

◆ Make sure all threads are fully engaged in tension controls.

◆ Use high-quality thread. Old or poor-quality thread can lead to thread breakage, skipped stitches, tension glitches, and inconsistent stitch formation.

◆ For rolled edges that don't roll: Increase the stitch width, or use a strip of water-soluble stabilizer over the edge.

◆ Clean and oil (unless it's self-oiling) your machine often, according to the manual instructions. Have it dealer serviced and cleaned annually.

Serger Company Contacts

Contact the following companies for product information and dealer referrals:

Baby Lock U.S.A, 1760 Gilsinn Lane, Fenton, MO 63026, phone (800) 422-2952, fax (314) 349-2333. web site www.babylock.com. Baby Lock.

Bernina of America, 3500 Thayer Court, Aurora, IL 60504-6182, phone (800) 405-2SEW (dealer referrals only), (630) 978-2500, fax (630) 978-8214, e-mail questions @usa.bernina.com. web site www.berninausa.com. Bernina, Bernette, Funlock.

Brother International Corp., 100 Somerset Corporate Blvd., Bridgewater, NJ 08807-0911, phone (908) 704-1700, fax (908) 575-3721. web site www.brother.com. Brother, Homelock. (Also makes models for other manufacturers.)

Elna USA, 1760 Gilsinn Lane, Fenton, MO 63036, phone (800) 848-ELNA, e-mail elnahelp@mindspring.com. web site www.elnausa.com. Elna.

Jaguar/JIC Inc., 1013 South Boulevard., Oak Park, IL 60302, phone (800) 959-5421, fax (708) 524-1913. Epochlock.

Juki, 14518 Best Ave., Sante Fe Springs, CA 90670, phone (562) 483-5355, fax (562) 404-4194. Juki.

Necchi/Allyn International, 1075 Santa Fe Drive, Denver, CO 80204, phone (800) 525-9987, fax (303) 825-5078. e-mail necchi@allynint.com. web site www.allynint.com. Necchi.

Nelco, 164 W. 25th Street, New York, NY 10001, phone (800) 221-8284, fax (212) 633-6380. Nelco.

New Home/Janome, 10 Industrial Avenue, Mahwah, NJ 07430, phone (800) 631-0183, fax (201) 825-1488. MyLock, Compulock.

Pfaff America, P.O. Box 566, Paramus, NJ 07653, phone (800) 99PFAFF, fax (201) 262-0696. web site www.pfaff-us-cda.com. Hobbylock.

Riccar America, 1800 E. Walnut Avenue, Fullerton, CA 92831, phone (800) 995-9110, fax (714) 525-3200. web site www.riccar.com. Riccar.

Simplicity Sewing Machines, P.O. Box 730, Fenton, MO 63026, phone (800) 335-0025. Easy Lock.

Sears, Sears Tower, Chicago, IL 60684. Kenmore.

Singer Sewing Co., 4500 Singer Road, Murfreesborg, TN 37129, phone (800) 474-6437, fax (615) 893-3061. Quantumlock, Ultralock.

Viking Sewing Machines Inc., 3100 Viking Parkway, Westlake, OH 44145, phone (800) 358-0001. www.husqvarnaviking.com. Huskylock.

White Sewing Machine Co., 3100 Viking Parkway, Westlake, OH 44145, phone (800) 358-0001. Superlock, Speedylock.

Baby Lock

Ann Riegel, Baby Lock National Communications Director

◆ When a seam spreads, don't assume the needle thread tension needs to be tightened. Spreading of the seamline, or "laddering," could be caused by too-tight looper tensions pulling on the needle thread **(A)**. Try loosening the loopers slightly.

(A)

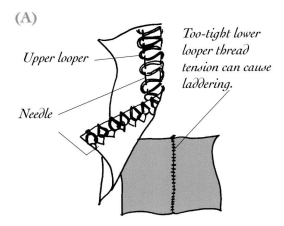

Upper looper

Too-tight lower looper thread tension can cause laddering.

Needle

◆ To prevent laddering on a 3/4-thread stitch: Adjust the right needle tension slightly looser than the left needle tension **(B)**. If the right needle thread is too tight, it can pull on the left needle thread, pulling open the seamline.

(B)

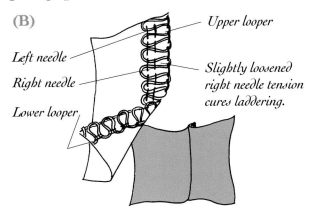

Left needle

Right needle

Lower looper

Upper looper

Slightly loosened right needle tension cures laddering.

◆ Know your thread. Top-quality, name-brand thread will break less and produce fewer skipped stitches. Color also makes a difference: Heavily dyed threads—dark shades and black—are generally more difficult to use than white or beige.

◆ For the most predictable results, use a consistent brand, weight, and type of thread in all positions (applicable to basic seaming and finishing).

Kelly Latreille, Baby Lock National Education Manager

◆ Follow these threading tips when using our "Jet Air" feature:

✧ If a decorative thread is too limp or fine (rayon, metallic, monofilament-nylon, woolly stretch nylon) to feed through easily, tie on a section of all-purpose thread and then pump it through the looper eye.

✧ Use a 20" to 30" thread cradle of serger or all-purpose thread and jet-air the strands through the looper. Insert decorative thread into the thread-cradle loop and pull through the looper.

✧ For heavier decorative threads, use our specially designed looper threader as shown **(C)**.

(C) *Decorative thread strategy:*

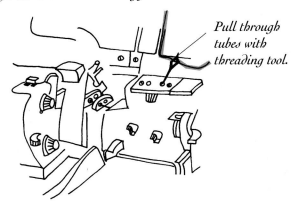

Pull through tubes with threading tool.

◆ If lightweight fabrics, such as silks and silk-likes, aren't feeding correctly, check the knives. Dull blades will cause a drag on the fabric feed.

◆ To decrease stretching when serging thin, lightweight silkies or tricots, move the differential feed up one notch or to a plus-setting.

Sharon Sullivan, Baby Lock National Communications Coordinator

◆ To prevent twisting and breakage, use a Horizontal Thread Holder for flat threads such as tinsel metallic and ribbon floss (see page 74).

Bernina (Bernette, Funlock)

Agnes Mercik, Bernina Promotions and Training Consultant

◆ For surefire results, approach serger troubleshooting step-by-step:

1. Check for proper sequence and path of all threading positions.

2. Make sure the threads are fully engaged in the tension controls. To do this, loosen tensions to "0" while rethreading. On some of our models, completely loosening or "releasing" the tensions is done by simply raising the presser foot.

3. Balance and adjust the looper tensions first, then the needle tensions.

4. Inspect the needle for dullness and damage (see page 15). Remember, synthetic fibers will dull needles more quickly than natural fibers.

◆ Match stripes and plaids by offsetting the lower layer slightly to the right—about ¹⁄₁₆". Then serge, trimming the under layer **(A)**.

(A)

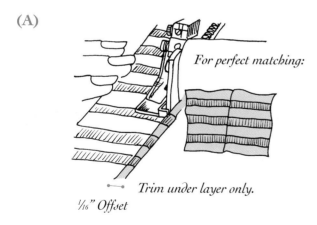

For perfect matching:

Trim under layer only.

¹⁄₁₆" Offset

◆ Coordinate your fabric/thread and your needle: Woven fabrics—"sharps" needles; densely woven fabrics—jeans, Microtex/Sharp, or quilting needles; knits—ballpoint needles; decorative threads—topstitching, embroidery or Metalfil needles; stubborn leathers and suedes—leather needles.

◆ To prevent breakage, stick with good-quality thread, particularly for stitches requiring tight tensions (rolled edges, wrapped seams or edges, or 3-thread flatlocking).

◆ When you need a tighter tension than provided by tension controls, use woolly stretch nylon. This thread stretches as it passes through the guides and eyes, increasing the tension by 2 to 3 settings.

◆ Test-serge: Heavily dyed threads—intense shades and black—may require tighter tensions.

◆ Favorite tips for narrow rolled edging:

◇ Let the knife trim at least a small amount from the edge.

◇ For enhanced tension tightening, use woolly stretch nylon in the lower looper (of a 3-thread) or the needle (of a 2-thread).

◇ For a cleaner, ravel-free finish, place a strip of water-soluble stabilizer over the fabric edge before serging.

◇ Roll and fuse: Press a ½"-wide strip of paper-backed fusible web to the wrong side of the edge. Remove the paper. Right side up, serge along the edge, trimming off about ⅜" (⅛" of the fusible will remain). Steam and press to set the roll **(B)**.

(B)

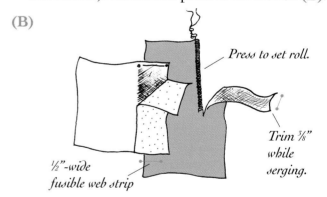

Press to set roll.

½"-wide fusible web strip

Trim ⅜" while serging.

◇ To serge straighter and more uniformly when finishing lightweight fabrics, serge on and off the edge over a scrap-fabric "bridge" **(C)**.

(C)

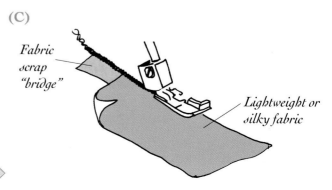

Fabric scrap "bridge"

Lightweight or silky fabric

Brother (Homelock)

Keri Morales, Brother Sewing Consultant

◆ Tension tips:

✧ After threading, give a "love tug" below and above the tension controls to make certain the threads are fully engaged (A).

(A)

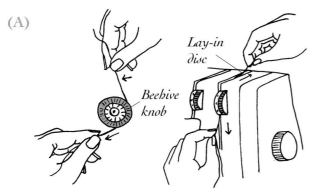

"Love tug" fully engages thread in tension control.

✧ Clean out the tension controls (trapped lint can prevent threads from seating properly). First, loosen tensions completely. Then pull a soft strip of cloth back and forth between the control discs (B).

(B)

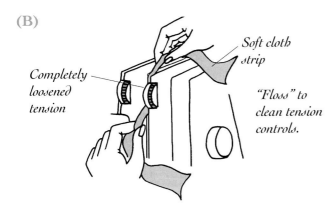

"Floss" to clean tension controls.

◆ If the thread is too loopy, increase the stitch width first (see pages 20-21), then tighten the looper tensions. Be careful not to widen or tighten too much; doing so can cause tunneling.

◆ Thread tips:

✧ Blend threads to subdue the "striping" that results when variegated thread is used in the looper(s). Either blend two strands of the same variegated shade, or blend a strand of variegated with a strand of solid color thread (see pages 46-47, 74, 76).

✧ Opt for long-fiber, synthetic thread. It's durable for high-stress, high-speed serging and leaves less fuzz and residue in your machine.

◆ Cleaning tips:

✧ Treat your machine to an annual dealer cleaning. As a reminder each year, take it in when you start spring cleaning at home.

✧ Use compressed air, or small specialized vacuum cleaners (sold at dealerships). Avoid standard vacuum cleaners, because they can actually "inhale" parts of the serger.

✧ For thorough cleaning, remove the presser foot, disengage the knives and remove the throat plate.

✧ Oil with Teflon® oil, sold at machine dealers. Oil where metal meets metal—usually four main locations on the machine (see page 90). Follow the oiling guidelines outlined in your manual.

✧ Oil self-lubricating sergers if they haven't been used for a while (the machine needs to run in order for the parts to self-lubricate).

✧ Once a month, remove the underside casing of your serger. Just a couple of screws hold it in place (C). If unsure, consult with your dealer about how to remove it. Wash it off with soap and water.

(C)

Unscrew, remove, and wash underside casing.

Elna (Elna Lock)

**Jane Burbach, Elna Education Director;
Larry Diekman, Manager of Technical Services**

◆ Troubleshoot tension problems:

◇ Study the tension controls. Are the threads fully engaged?

◇ Look for lint or debris caught between the discs, preventing the thread from engaging completely (see pages 57, 60, 90).

◇ Don't confuse tension settings with stitch width adjustments. "Tunneling," does not always mean the looper tensions are too tight; often this is indicative of width set too wide for the stitch and the fabric **(A)**.

(A)

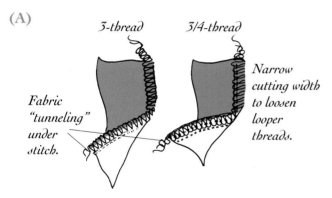

3-thread   3/4-thread

Narrow cutting width to loosen looper threads.

Fabric "tunneling" under stitch.

◆ Troubleshoot stitch formation problems:

◇ Study the thread path, searching for bypassed guides.

◇ Inspect the needle, presser foot, throat plate, and loopers for burrs (see page 15).

◇ Persistent stitch formation problems may be due to a bent looper. Take your machine in for servicing.

◆ Troubleshoot threading problems:

◇ Take time to learn how to thread your model. Repetition is the best teacher. The more you thread your serger, the easier and more mistake-proof it will become.

◇ Don't bypass the thread clamp or guide directly above the needles.

◆ Troubleshoot thread problems:

◇ Use high-quality, name-brand thread.

◇ Change needle size and type for decorative threads and specialty fabrics (see page 84).

◇ Guarantee smooth, even thread flow when using slippery rayon and metallic threads: Use thread nets and place the foam pads under heavier decorative thread cones to prevent bouncing and tangling underneath.

◇ To decrease tension on decorative threads, use our tension-release clips **(B)**.

(B)

To additionally decrease tension, use the pre-tension release clip.

◆ Troubleshoot needle problems:

◇ Use the correct needle for the fabric, thread, and technique. For Elna sergers, we recommend ELx705 needles, sizes 12/80 and 14/90. If you run out, or are serging on specialty fabric or thread, use the specialty needle designed for that purpose (see page 84).

◇ Insert the needle all the way into the shaft, and align it properly (see pages 28-29). Elna sergers have a separate set-screw for each needle position.

◆ Troubleshoot cutting problems:

◇ Remove lint that has built up between the lower and upper blades.

◇ Correctly set the height of the lower blade; it should be even with the throat plate (see page 32).

◆ Troubleshoot maintenance problems:

◇ Once a year, have your serger cleaned and serviced by your dealer. There are many inaccessible areas that collect lint and oil.

Juki

Nel Howard and Betty Quinell, Juki Sales Representatives/Educational Coordinators

◆ Think of tension controls as speed regulators: If thread is feeding through too fast, it will be too loose in the stitch.

Note: Juki tensions are single rotation. Generally, a setting of "4" on all Juki controls will result in a balanced-tension stitch.

◆ Although any household needle will work in our current sergers, use Organ brand household needles for the best results. Most Oriental machines are timed for needles made in the Orient, such as the Organ brand.

◆ Turn the light on when threading the needle. This "back light" shines through the eye, simplifying correct positioning and threading. For optimum light, raise the needle bar to its highest position. Also, for easy threading, use the wire loop needle threader provided in the accessory kit (A).

(A)

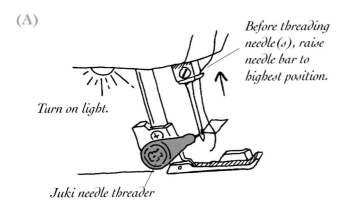

Turn on light.

Before threading needle(s), raise needle bar to highest position.

Juki needle threader

◆ Remember that lint is the enemy. We recommend a thorough cleaning before oiling.

◆ Every six to eight months, remove the throat plate and brush lint from between the feed dogs. Excess lint can impair feeding.

◆ Use the small brush supplied in your accessory kit for cleaning tight areas. For larger areas, buy a stenciling or makeup brush. Dampen the end very lightly with oil so that it attracts more lint.

◆ For smooth stitching action, place two drops of oil on the looper elbows prior to each serging session (B).

(B)

Lightly oil looper elbows.

◆ If your narrow rolled edge won't roll:

  ◇ Try gradually lengthening your stitch.

  ◇ Try moving your lower knife to the right, widening the bite and the amount of fabric inside the stitch.

  ◇ Try the left needle position—possible on Jukis, but not all sergers—when using heavier or stubborn fabrics.

  ◇ If using metallic thread in the upper looper (of a 3-thread) or looper (of a 2-thread), and the edge does not roll completely, try finger-rolling the edge after serging.

◆ Watch serged seam widths. Most looper-cover seam guides are gauged for an "average" stitch and seam width. If you move the knives, the gauge becomes inaccurate. (A narrow ⅛" change in seam allowance width can equate to a full size change in a four-seam garment.)

◆ Be aware that serger knives cut the fabric edge before the stitch is formed. On Jukis, for instance, the knife cuts ½" in front of the needles (this distance varies on other models). For accuracy, keep your eye on the knives. When serging curves, however, watch the needle and straighten the edge in front of the knives.

Necchi/Allyn International

Tom Johnson, Necchi/Allyn International Head Technician

◆ For normal tension settings on most Necchi sergers, dial to a "3" setting on all controls (needles and loopers).

◆ If you forget to close the looper cover before serging, and trimmings fall into the looper area, causing jamming: Stop. Don't try to pull away the fabric and threads, which can also pull the loopers out of alignment. Instead, cut away the tangled threads and fabric **(A)**.

(A)

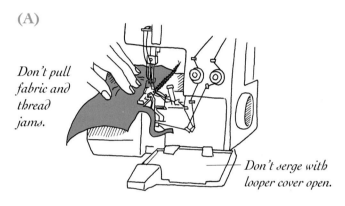

Don't pull fabric and thread jams.

Don't serge with looper cover open.

◆ Oil your serger **(B)**. If your serger doesn't have an oiling wick on top, take it to your dealer at least once a year to have the main shaft oiled. Failure to do so may cause the machine to bind, requiring disassembly and repair.

(B)

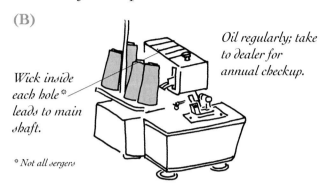

Wick inside each hole leads to main shaft.*

Oil regularly; take to dealer for annual checkup.

* Not all sergers

◆ Troubleshoot loopy needle thread: Check that the thread hasn't slipped behind the thread take-up lever, and/or fully engage the thread in the tension controls.

◆ Try widening the stitch slightly if your machine is not cutting. On some sergers, the knives can be set too far to the left, making a gap between the blades and thus preventing correct cutting action.

New Home/Janome (MyLock)

Sue Thornton-Gray, New Home Education Coordinator

◆ Clean out lay-in tension discs with a folded $1 (or $100?) bill. The oil on the bill will clean the tension discs and clean out any loose threads **(A)**. Also, a folded strip of soft cotton broadcloth will buff the discs, and remove thread-film buildup.

(A)

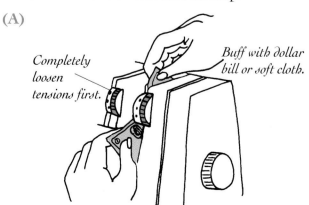

Completely loosen tensions first.

Buff with dollar bill or soft cloth.

◆ Check the sharpness of serger blades by serging a single layer of nylon tricot or silky polyester. If cutting is ragged, replace the lower knife blade (see pages 32-33).

◆ Use an old needle to clean debris from the feed-dogs **(B)**. (This is especially important for older sergers.)

(B)

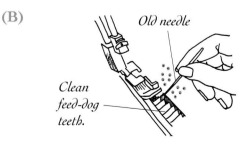

Old needle

Clean feed-dog teeth.

◆ Don't blow into your serger to remove lint. The moisture of your breath can cause rusting.

Pfaff (Hobbylock)

**Laura Haynie, Pfaff Education Manager;
Eileen Lenninger, Pfaff Educational Consultant**

◆ For creativity and accuracy, rely on accessory feet:

✧ Use our Lace Foot for serging pintucks. The moveable metal guide aligns the fabric exactly **(A)**.

(A) *Use lace foot for narrow, even pintucks.*

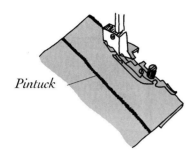

Pintuck

✧ Use our Blindhem Foot for flatlocking. Set the guide to eliminate cutting and ensure width uniformity. Also, when the stitches hang off the edge slightly, the flatlocking can be pulled flat **(B)**.

(B) *Use blindhem foot for flatlocking.*

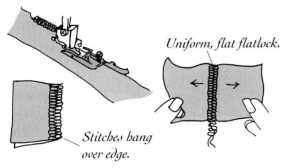

Uniform, flat flatlock.

Stitches hang over edge.

✧ Use our Cording Foot for zipper insertion. Align so that the zipper teeth ride in the groove underneath the foot **(C)**.

(C) *Use cording foot for zippers.*

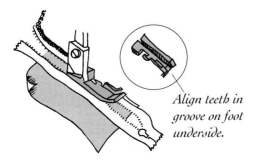

Align teeth in groove on foot underside.

✧ Use our Gimp Foot for wire-edged ribbons. Feed fine, spooled wire through the guide while serging **(D)**.

(D) *Use gimp foot for wire-edged ribbons.*

Fine wire

◆ If tying on needle threads and using serger thread, you can pull a tight square knot through the needle eye(s). Leave 1" tails after knotting **(E)**. To ease the knot through the eye, pull the thread down (under the foot) and to the back of the serger. If tying on looper threads, save time by tying an overhand knot instead of a square knot.

(E)

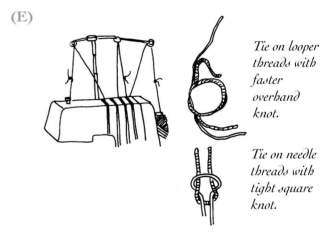

Tie on looper threads with faster overhand knot.

Tie on needle threads with tight square knot.

Walter Kwiatkowski, Pfaff Technician

◆ Clean your serger after each project. Use a lint brush and/or small vacuum cleaner.

◆ Save service fees and frustration by cleaning and oiling regularly.

◆ Oil frequently, but lightly. Too much oil can lock up your serger because it attracts lint to moving parts.

Singer (Quantumlock, Ultralock)

Singer Sewing Company Training and Education Department

◆ Place nets over decorative threads to prevent tangling. If the nets tighten the tension too much, make sure the net does not extend beyond the top of the cone or spool. Or, try cutting the nets in half to loosen the tension a bit more **(A)**.

(A)

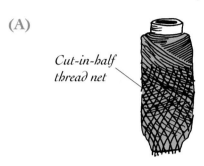

Cut-in-half thread net

◆ Place decorative thread spools, cones or ball skeins inside juice or jelly glasses behind the serger. The thread is contained and feeds uniformly **(B)**.

(B)

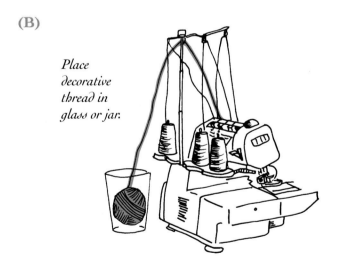

Place decorative thread in glass or jar.

◆ Before serging, pull all the threads above the throat plate while turning the handwheel clockwise about one-half a rotation. The reverse action slips the needle thread off the lower looper, preventing chronic needle-thread breakage.

◆ Prolong the life and performance of serger knives by cleaning carefully and frequently.

◆ When using the tie-on method to change thread (see page 12), remember to turn the tensions to zero before pulling the strands through. This prevents wear and tear on the discs **(C)**.

(C)

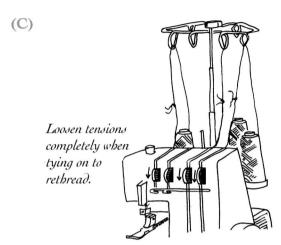

Loosen tensions completely when tying on to rethread.

◆ Find creative cleaning tools: A cotton ball held with serger tweezers works wonderfully to clean off oily, linty areas inside the machine **(D)**.

(D) *For lint removal:*

Cotton ball   *Serger tweezers*

◆ Fine-tune tensions by adjusting the stitch width. Widening the stitch tightens the looper tensions, while narrowing the stitch loosens them (see pages 8, 20-21, 22-23).

◆ To strengthen fragile metallic threads, blend with a strand of woolly stretch nylon (see pages 47, 74).

◆ Select the correct Singer Fabric Separator for the stitch type (see page 83). One is for the 3/4-thread overlock stitch, and one is for the 5-thread safety stitch. This specialty foot is perfect for gathering ruffles on a little girl's dress or country curtains.

◆ Note that some blind hem feet are designed for different fabric thicknesses. Select the correct blind hem foot for the weight or layers of fabric.

Viking (Huskylock)

**Sue Hausmann, host of America Sews (PBS);
Jim Suzio, Designer/Educator for
Viking Dealer Gloria Horn**

◆ When you first purchase a serger, allow enough time to get comfortable with it. Guaranteed, it will become your best sewing friend, and you'll wonder how you ever lived without it.

◆ Let the needle tensions guide you. I say, "The needle is the leader." This means that the tighter the needle tension, the tighter the other tensions need to be. Set the needle tension as loose as it can be for the desired technique, then adjust the looper tensions.

◆ Check the manual when adjusting for a rolled edge. On some Viking machines, you can use either the left or the right needle positions, whereas on others, only the left or the right.

◆ Leave the needle threaded when removing. If the needle slips into the serger, it can be quickly retrieved by pulling on the thread **(A)**.

(A)

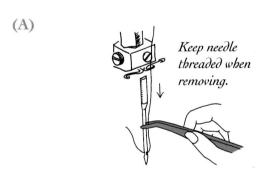

Keep needle threaded when removing.

◆ When tension is a problem, at least two threads are interacting. You have two choices: Either increase one tension or decrease the other, but don't adjust both at the same time.

◆ Release tension before threading your serger. (On many Huskylock models, automatic tension-release is as easy as raising the foot.) Doing so opens up the tension controls, ensuring that the threads will be completely seated.

Note: An indication of needle threads not fully seated in the tension controls is spreading seamlines (see page 39).

◆ When using small spools, remove the cone adapters from the thread stand and place the spools directly on the thread pins. (Thread can get caught in the adapters' grooves.) If the cone adapters are difficult to remove, apply a drop or two of oil to the thread pin, then try again **(B)**.

(B)

Remove cone adapter.

Add drop of oil for easy removal.

Place spool on thread pin.

◆ If your serger is jamming, make sure the fabric is feeding into the mouth of the knife blades **(C)**. Of course, the knives must be aligned properly and the upper knife in position for trimming.

(C)

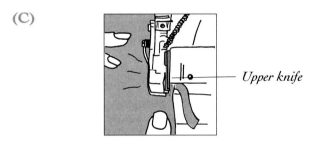

Upper knife

◆ If your threads are continually breaking, the problem may be that the telescopic thread guide isn't extended to the highest position **(D)**.

(D)

Carefully pull guide to highest position.

◆ Gently push the pointed end of your serger needle into a pink eraser. Then use the eraser as a handle to help insert or remove with ease.

White (Superlock, Speedylock)

Julie Davis, White Education Manager

◆ Take advantage of specialty needles to help prevent skipped stitches. We recommend size 11 or 14 Organ HAX1SP needles (sold by authorized White dealers) for Superlock models 534, 534D, 200-series, and 734.

◆ Heavy decorative thread takes up more room in the tension controls, therefore requiring lower (or looser) tensions. Finer threads take up less room, requiring higher (or tighter) tensions (A).

(A)

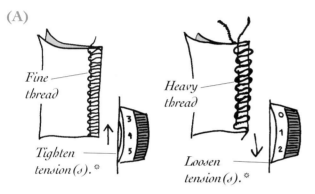

Fine thread

Tighten tension(s).*

Heavy thread

Loosen tension(s).*

* For most, but not all, sergers.

◆ Thread quality affects stitch quality (remember that higher price doesn't necessarily represent higher-quality thread). Look for smooth, long, continuous-filament thread, rather than threads with a "hairy" or uneven appearance (B).

(B)

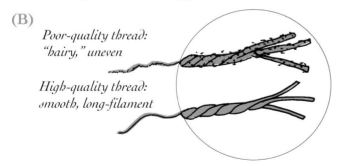

Poor-quality thread: "hairy," uneven

High-quality thread: smooth, long-filament

◆ To vary the amount of differential-feed gathering, adjust the stitch length. Longer stitches enhance gathering; shorter stitches may inhibit it.

◆ Remember that differential feed can be varied as you serge. For instance, when serging around an outside curve, adjust for a plus-setting to prevent stretching, then return to a normal setting along the straight edge.

◆ With rare exception, we don't suggest raising the "cutter" or upper knife. The cutting action allows the looper to pass over the fabric (C). Without the cutting action, the fabric might jam up on, and possibly damage, the looper.

(C)

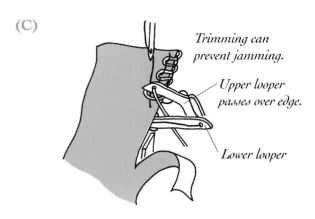

Trimming can prevent jamming.

Upper looper passes over edge.

Lower looper

Note: Some older White models have a fixed upper cutter/knife that cannot be disengaged, so you don't have to worry about serging without trimming.

◆ If you've forgotten the threading sequence for your serger or need a quick reminder of the paths, peek into the inside of the looper cover (D). Often the order and color-coded paths will be printed inside for at-a-glance, at-your-serger reference.

(D) *Threading order and paths printed inside serger.*

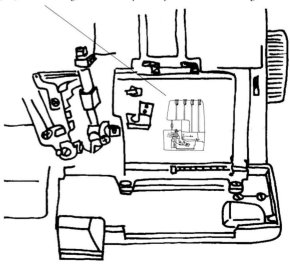

Sergers
Demystified

Sergers continue to improve and
advance our sewing.

And to keep you apprised of the
serging spectrum, we've
researched and compiled
comprehensive information about
sergers, stitches, and supplies.

◆

"Serger Models and Stitch
Capabilities" chart

◆

Definitions of serger models, plus
illustrations of stitches

◆

Dictionary of serging terms, notions

Chapter
3

Serger Models and Stitch Capabilities

Serger Model/Type	2/3-Thread	3-Thread	3/4-Thread	2/3/4-Thread	2/4-Thread*	2/3/4/5-Thread
2-Thread Overedge (A)	X	—	—	X	X	X**
2-Thread Flatlock (B)	X	—	—	X	X	X**
2-Thread Wrapped/ Seam (C)	X	—	—	X	X	X**
2-Thread Rolled Edge (D)	X	—	—	X	—	X**
2-Thread Chainstitch (E)	—	—	—	X**	X	X
3-Thread Overlock (F)	X	X	X	X	—	X
3-Thread Flatlock (G)	X	X	X	X	—	X
3-Thread Wrapped (H)	X	X	X	X	—	X
3-Thread Rolled Edge (I)	X	X	X	X	—	X
3-Thread Cover Hem/Stitch (J)	—	—	—	X**	—	X**
4-Thread Overlock (K)	—	—	X	X	—	X
4-Thread Safety Stitch (L)	—	—	—	—	X	X**
4-Thread Mock Safety Stitch (M)	—	—	X	X	—	X**
5-Thread Safety Stitch (N)	—	—	—	—	—	X

*2/4-thread sergers are not readily available. Check local dealers or classified ads in sewing publications and newspapers.

**Some, but not all, models.

Note: This chart was verified for accuracy during each of the many proofing stages of this book. However, due to constant changes in the serger market (and although information is updated with each reprinting), there may be additions and corrections after publication. For up-to-the-minute information about model specifications and stitch capabilities, visit your local sewing machine dealerships. Also see pages 78-79.

Serger Models Defined

2/3-Thread: One needle and two loopers for 2- or 3-thread serging.

3-Thread: One needle and two loopers for 3-thread serging.

3/4-Thread: Two needles and two loopers for 3- or 4-thread serging.

2/3/4-Thread: Two needles and two loopers for 2-, 3-, or 4-thread serging.

2/4-Thread: Two needles and two loopers for 2- or 4-thread serging.

2/3/4/5-Thread: Three needles and three loopers for 2-, 3-, 4-, or 5-thread serging.

Stitches Illustrated

(A) 2-Thread Overedge	Looper / Needle
(H) 3-Thread Wrapped	Upper looper / Needle / Lower looper
(B) 2-Thread Flatlock	Looper / Needle
(I) 3-Thread Rolled Edge	Upper looper / Needle / Lower looper
(C) 2-Thread Wrapped/Seam	Needle / Looper
(J) 3-Thread Cover Hem/Stitch	Left needle / Right needle / Looper
(D) 2-Thread Rolled Edge	Needle / Looper
(K) 4-Thread Overlock	Left needle / Right needle / Upper looper / Lower looper
(E) 2-Thread Chainstitch	Chainstitch needle / Chainstitch looper
(L) 4-Thread Safety Stitch	Chainstitch needle / Right needle / Chainstitch looper / Upper looper
(F) 3-Thread Overlock	Upper looper / Needle / Lower looper
(M) 4-Thread Mock Safety Stitch	Left needle / Right needle / Lower looper / Upper looper
(G) 3-Thread Flatlock	Upper looper / Lower looper / Needle
(N) 5-Thread Safety Stitch	Chainstitch needle / Needle / Chainstitch looper / Upper looper / Lower looper

Jargon: Your Serger Dictionary

We occasionally confuse our readers with "serger-eze," a language only sewing journalists understand. We hope the following definitions will translate any foreign language you find in this book. Note that two sections follow: First, "Terms," then "Notions," each alphabetized respectively.

TERMS:

Balance wheel: See "Handwheel."

Balanced-tension serging: On 3- or 3/4-thread overlocking—upper looper thread exposed on stitch top side, lower looper thread exposed on stitch underside, with both interlocking at stitch edge. On 2-thread overedging—looper thread exposed only on stitch top side, needle thread exposed on stitch underside, with both interlocking at stitch edge. On 2-thread chainstitching—needle thread exposed on stitch top side, looper thread exposed on stitch underside. Also see pages 8-9.

Balanced stitch: See "Balanced-tension serging" above, and pages 8-9.

Beehive knobs: One variety of tension controls, consisting of round knobs that protrude from serger front. Turn right to tighten, left to loosen **(A)**.

(A)

Left to loosen

Right to tighten

Beehive knobs

Bite: Amount of fabric within stitch (also referred to as "stitch width").

Blades: See "Knives," page 70.

Blanket stitch: Of the several serged blanket-stitching methods, one easy approach is serge-finishing wrong side up with a 2- or 3-thread flatlock, using decorative thread in the needle. The needle thread forms the "blanket" stitches on the fabric's right side **(B)**.

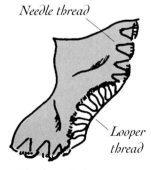

(B)

Needle thread

Looper thread

Blanket stitch

Blind hem: A near-invisible hemming technique that hems and serge-finishes in one step. For effortless, accurate guiding, use a blind hem foot (see page 81).

Burying chain tails: Used to secure beginning/end of serged stitch. Achieved by threading chain tail through tapestry needle, double-eyed transfer needle, or loop turner, then burying it within the serging **(C)**.

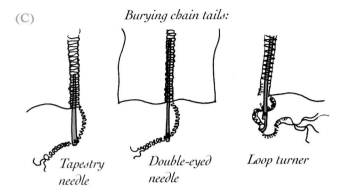

(C)

Burying chain tails:

Tapestry needle

Double-eyed needle

Loop turner

Chain tails: Serged thread that forms chain effect before serging on, and after serging off, fabric. Also see "Chaining off," below, and "Thread chain," page 74.

Chaining off: Serging without fabric at end of serge-seaming or serge-finishing, or simply serging without fabric underneath to create thread chain (also called "serging on air").

Chainstitch: See pages 8, 24, 66-67.

Clearing stitch finger: Removing stitches from stitch finger. If available, activate tension-release. Raise presser foot and turn handwheel until needle is in highest position, pulling finger-width of slack in needle thread, then gently pull thread chain toward back of serger until stitches slide off finger **(D)**.

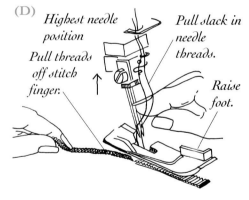

(D)

Highest needle position

Pull slack in needle threads.

Pull threads off stitch finger.

Raise foot.

Combi: New Home/Janome-brand machine featuring a 2-thread serger one side, and a conventional sewing machine on other side.

Conventional sewing machine: A straight stitch (or "lockstitch") sewing machine.

Converter: Used for 2-thread serging (on 2/3-, 2/3/4- and some 5-thread sergers), this small mechanism (an accessory, or built-in) is located next to upper looper and fills in upper looper eye.

Corded edge: Serge-finishing over a filler cord(s) for a stable, more defined edge **(E)**.

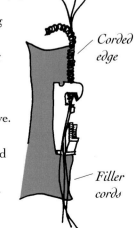

(E)

Corded edge

Filler cords

Cover hem/cover stitch: See pages 9, 66-67.

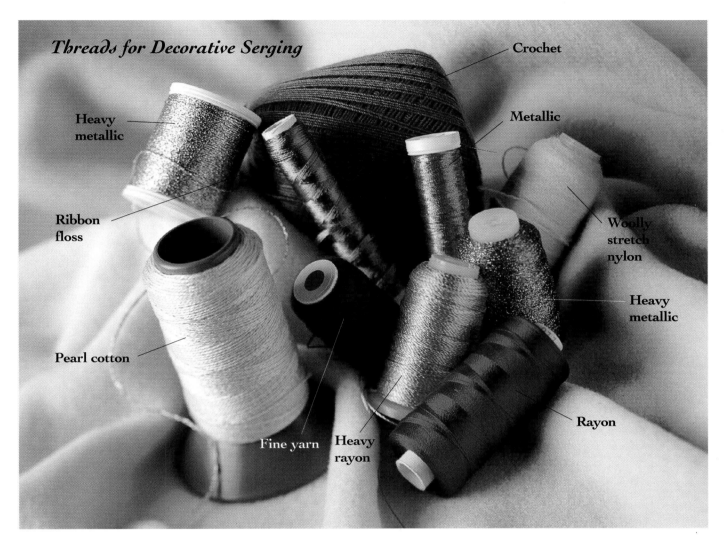

Threads for Decorative Serging

Crochet

Heavy metallic

Metallic

Ribbon floss

Woolly stretch nylon

Pearl cotton

Heavy metallic

Fine yarn

Heavy rayon

Rayon

Cover stitch machine: Special machine, such as the Morita® , that features only the cover hem/stitch (see pages 66-67).

Cross-wound: The direction in which serger (and some decorative) thread is wound onto cones so it feeds easily and evenly when pulled upward **(F)**.

Cutting width: A lower-knife adjustment that moves independently from the stitch finger, fine-tuning the fabric width under the looper threads to perfect the stitch.

Decorative serging: Exposed serging, using decorative, serger, or all-purpose thread. See pages 46-49, 85-87.

Differential feed: Two sets of feed dogs (one front, one back) that work together at the same or different rates

(F) *Cross-wound thread*

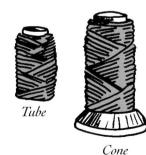

Tube

Cone

(G). Can work at 1:1 ratio (a "1" or "N" setting indicates the same amount of fabric taken in as being released) for basic serging. Can be adjusted to prevent stretching, enhance gathering, and assist in easing (above a "1" setting—see "Plus-setting," page 72). Can be adjusted to prevent puckering or enhance lettucing (below a "1" setting—see "Minus-setting," page 71).

(G) *Differential feed:*

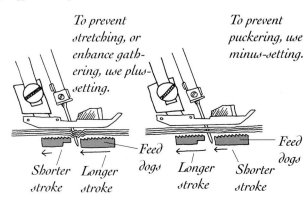

To prevent stretching, or enhance gathering, use plus-setting.

To prevent puckering, use minus-setting.

Feed dogs

Feed dogs

Shorter stroke *Longer stroke*

Longer stroke *Shorter stroke*

Ease-plusing: Manual means of achieving a differential feed plus-setting. Use your right hand to force fabric under the presser foot, and your left hand to slow its exit from behind the presser foot (see page 37).

Edge finishing: See "Serge-finish," page 72.

Electronic foot control: Provides full needle penetration and cutting at any serging speed.

Feed dogs: Extending slightly above throat plate and beneath presser foot, these side-by-side strips of slightly protruding "teeth" move fabric under the foot. *Note:* The teeth move up and down with the needle, moving the fabric when the needle is up.

Flatbed insert: Accessory piece that's inserted flush with throat plate to cover knives and assist in 2-thread chainstitch-topstitching and 3-thread cover hemming/stitching (no trimming). Feature on some, but not all sergers with chainstitch capability. Also called "material guide plate" and "sewing table" (H).

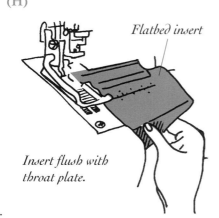

(H)

Flatbed insert

Insert flush with throat plate.

Flatlock/flatlock stitch: See pages 44-45, 66-67.

Flywheel: See "Handwheel," right.

Foot pedal/control: Controls starting, stopping, and speed of serging.

Foot pressure: Amount of weight presser foot exerts onto fabric. Adjustable, using a screw or lever (I).

(I) *Foot pressure:*

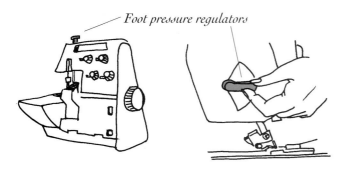

Foot pressure regulators

Free-arm: Small work surface on some sergers that accommodates serging tubular pieces more easily. A detachable work area converts surface from flatbed to free-arm.

Groove: See "Needle groove," page 72.

Hairy edges: Small, raveling fabric threads that protrude from a serge-finished edge (most commonly on rolled edges). Also called "pokies." (See pages 16-17.)

Handwheel: Located on right-hand side of serger, it turns toward machine front (same as conventional sewing machines) to raise/lower needle and create stitches manually. *Note:* On some older models, handwheel turns in opposite direction. Also called "flywheel."

Hiccup: An area within serging where the stitch has narrowed, then returned to its consistent width (J).

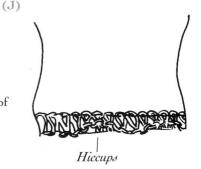

(J)

Hiccups

Knife guard: Portion of looper cover that conceals knives, protecting user from coming into contact with them, as well as fabric trimmings from becoming tangled in loopers.

Knife mouth: Area between upper and lower knife blades into which fabric enters for cutting. (See page 32.)

Knives: Serger's cutting mechanism, consisting of two knifelike blades. Upper blade moves in up-and-down motion; lower blade is stationary. Most upper blades can be disengaged for no-trim serging.

Ladders: On pulled-flat flatlock seam, exposed needle thread in sequence of horizontal stitches. (See pages 44-45.)

Lay-in discs: One variety of tension controls that are incorporated into— almost flush against—serger front. Dial up to tighten, down to loosen*. Also called "inlaid tension controls" (K).

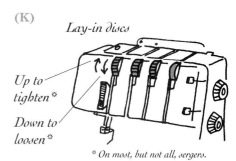

(K)

Lay-in discs

Up to tighten*

Down to loosen*

* On most, but not all, sergers.

LCD: Liquid crystal display. One variety of stitch display screens (see "Stitch display screen," page 72).

LED: Light emitting diode. One variety of stitch display screens (see "Stitch display screen," page 72).

Lettucing: Rippled or ruffled finish created on stretchy

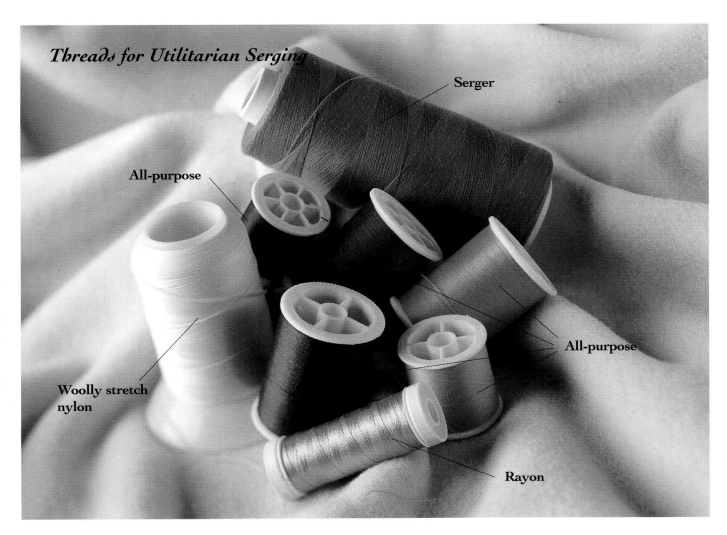

Threads for Utilitarian Serging

Serger

All-purpose

Woolly stretch nylon

All-purpose

Rayon

edges (usually **(L)** cross-grain knits or bias-cut wovens), using a short, rolled or balanced stitch, and stretching fabric gently in front of and behind presser foot. Differential feed at minus-setting enhances effect **(L)**.

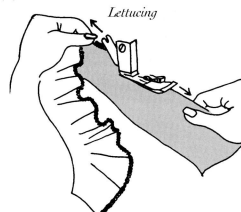

Lettucing

Looper cover: Front "door" of serger that can be opened to expose loopers and thread guides. Some sergers will not operate with looper cover open.

Loopers: Metal, large-eyed mechanisms (one upper, right; and one lower, left) within each serger. Threads used in loopers interlock with needle thread and with each other at edge to create "knitting" process. Looper eyes can accommodate heavyweight thread and fine yarns.

Note: Some sergers, such as 2/4- and 5-thread models, feature an additional chainstitch looper that, when threaded, interlocks with the chainstitch needle thread to create a serged chainstitch. Also, some 3/4- and 5-thread sergers can make a cover hem/stitch using chainstitch or lower looper. See further explanation on pages 66-67.

Loops: On a balanced-tension stitch, flatlocked stitch, or cover hem/stitch, the exposed thread "squiggles" produced by the looper thread(s).

Manual stitches: Using your hand, rather than foot pedal, to turn handwheel and form stitches. Also called "advancing by hand."

Material guide plate: See "Flatbed insert," page 70.

Minus-setting: A below-"N" (normal), or "1" (down to "0.5") differential feed setting. Stretches fabric slightly to ensure smooth seams and edges (balanced and rolled), especially in woven fabrics that tend to pucker. Also enhances manual stretching for lettuced effects.

Mock safety stitch: See pages 66-67.

Mouth: See "Knife mouth," page 70.

Needle bar: Metal cylinder onto which serger needle clamp fits **(M)**.

Needle clamp: Small metal unit into which serger needle is inserted **(M)**.

(M)

Needle clamp *Needle bar*

Needle groove: Long slot on needle front (above eye) in which thread lies. Always to front of machine when needle is inserted properly.

Needle holder: See "Needle clamp," above.

Needle plate: See "Throat plate," page 74.

Needle scarf: Short indentation on needle back (above eye). Always to back of machine when needle is inserted properly.

Needle shaft: See "Needle bar," above.

Needle shank: Upper portion of needle that's inserted into needle clamp.

Overedge: See pages 8, 66-67.

Overlock: See pages 9, 66-67.

Plus-setting: An above-"N" (normal), or "1" (up to "2.25") differential feed setting. Draws up fabric for gathering and easing, plus ribbing and elastic application.

Pokies: See "Hairy edges," page 70.

Presser foot lift: Used to raise/lower the presser foot. Located on back side of machine to the left, or on front of machine to right of looper cover. Also called "sewing foot lever." Available as knee lift on some sergers.

Presser-foot pressure dial: See "Foot pressure," page 70.

Rolled-edge stitch/rolled hem: See pages 42-43, 66-67.

Safety stitch: Chainstitch. Also see pages 66-67.

Satin-length stitch: Dense serged stitch that creates satiny, filled-in finish. Accomplished with a short stitch length using fine thread, and with a slightly longer stitch length using heavy thread.

Scarf: See "Needle scarf," above.

Seated: Engaged, i.e., thread engaged in tension mechanism (beehive knob or lay-in disc).

Securing seams: See "Burying chain tails" (page 68), "Loop turner" (page 75) and "Seam sealant" (page 75).

Serge-finish: Serging along fabric's raw edge to create clean, even, ravel-free finish. **(N)**

Serge-seam: Serging to join two or more fabric layers **(N)**.

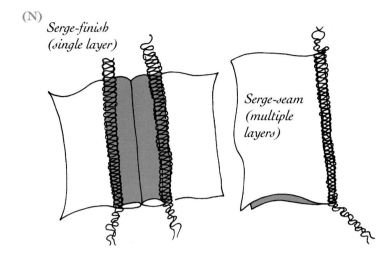

(N)
Serge-finish (single layer) *Serge-seam (multiple layers)*

Serger knives: See "Knives," page 70.

Set-screw: Tiny screw that secures needle in serger's needle clamp **(O)**.

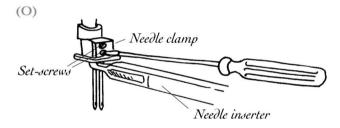

(O)
Needle clamp *Set-screws* *Needle inserter*

Shank: See "Needle shank," left.

Shirring: Gathering. Easiest using differential feed at highest plus-setting. To enhance gathering, lengthen stitch and tighten needle tension(s). Using a shirring foot and differential plus-setting can simultaneously shirr light-to-medium weight fabric and attach it to flat top layer (see page 80).

Speed/speed control: Sergers can sew (serge) approximately 1,500 stitches per minute (spm). Some machines feature two or three speed options for slower serging, too.

SPM: Stitches per minute (speed).

Stitch display screen: Electronic screen on some serger fronts displaying information about stitches, tensions, etc. Also see "LCD" and "LED" (see page 70).

Stitch finger: Metal prong, located within throat plate or on presser foot, around which serged stitches are formed.

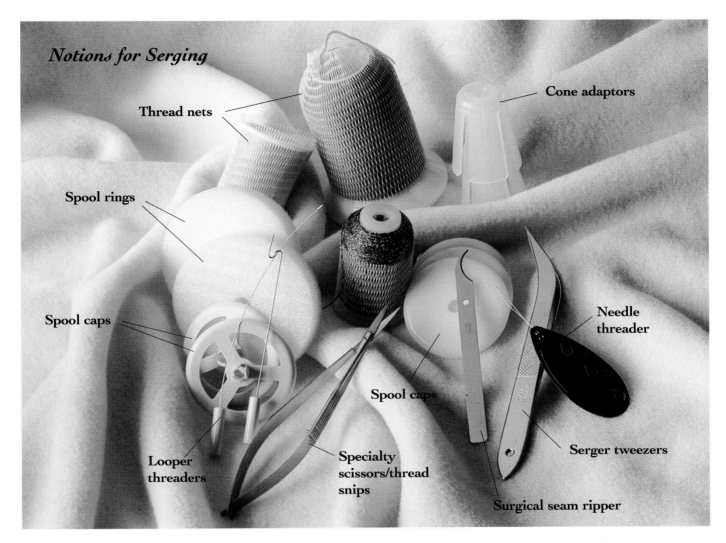

Notions for Serging

- Thread nets
- Cone adaptors
- Spool rings
- Spool caps
- Needle threader
- Spool caps
- Looper threaders
- Specialty scissors/thread snips
- Serger tweezers
- Surgical seam ripper

Stitch length: Vertical distance in millimeters between needle penetration points. Generally ranging from close satin-length (1mm or less) to airy (4mm to 5mm).

Stitch width: Horizontal distance in millimeters between needle thread and right edge of serged stitch. Generally from 1mm (narrow) to 7.5mm to 9mm (wide). Manipulated by stitch width knob, needle position and/or knife position, depending on serger brand/model (P).

Taut-serging: Manual means of achieving a differential feed minus-setting. While serging, hold fabric gently taut in front of and behind presser foot (see page 35).

Telescopic thread guide: Extensions of the thread guides located to the back of serger. Features first guides threads pass through as they come off spools or cones. Needs to be fully extended for trouble-free serging (see page 63).

Tension dials/discs: See "Beehive knobs" (page 68) and "Lay-in discs" (page 70).

Tension release: A control that releases all tensions so

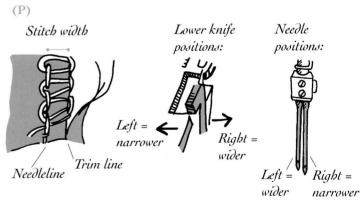

(P)

Stitch width

Lower knife positions:

Needle positions:

Left = narrower *Right = wider*

Left = wider *Right = narrower*

Needleline *Trim line*

thread can be pulled through effortlessly. Activated by separate mechanism or automatically when presser foot is lifted. Not on all brands/models.

Tension: Controls thread flow through beehive knobs or lay-in discs. Adjusted for different fabrics, threads, stitches.

Thread chain: Serged loops formed by serging without fabric. Also see "Chain tails," page 68.

Thread cutter: Small, protected cutting edge attached to serger behind presser foot (or attached to presser foot shank). Used to cut chain tail after serging.

Thread guides: Metal eyes, hooks, and discs between thread cone/spool and its respective needle or looper eye, through which threads pass. Most serger models are color-coded for easy path identification and threading.

Threading path: Area along which each thread travels from cone/spool to needle or looper eye.

Thread pins: Vertical posts attached to serger's thread stand for holding thread cones or spools. Also called "thread rods."

Thread stand: Base at back of serger where thread pins are located. Also called "spool stand."

Thread-blending: Combining two or more threads (novelty and/or all-purpose) through one looper for unique decorative effects. Use Thread Palette (see page 76) for glitch-free blending.

Threading sequence: Most sergers must be threaded in a specific order (usually, but not always—upper looper, lower looper, needle) for successful serging. Check manual.

Throat plate: Metal plate below presser foot, surrounding feed dogs and stitch finger and incorporated into serger's flat bed **(Q)**. Also called "stitch plate" or "needle plate."

Timing: The exact setting or placement of loopers and needles for a machine to sew a serged stitch. "Repair" that must be made by a mechanic certified to work on your serger brand.

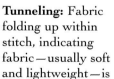

(Q)

Throat plate

Tunneling: Fabric folding up within stitch, indicating fabric—usually soft and lightweight—is buckling under stitch, or looper tensions are too tight. (See pages 20-21, 58.)

Wrapped stitch: See pages 43, 66-67.

NOTIONS:

Accessory feet: Generally optional (some are included with some sergers) presser feet or attachments to assist in special serging tasks. Examples: beading/pearl foot, blind hem foot, cording foot, elasticator foot, gimp foot, shirring foot, and more). See pages 80-83.

All-purpose thread: See page 86.

Canned air: Direct airstream in a can. Used to clean lint and dust from serger. Choose ozone-friendly variety; some now also moisture-free. Also called "compressed air."

Crocus Cloth: Denim fabric impregnated with a fine buffing compound. Used to smooth burrs on loopers and rough spots on throat plates.

Double-eyed transfer needle: Long (about 3½"), double-eyed, blunt "needle" used for burying chain tails.

Extension table: See "Serger table," page 76.

Filler cord: One or more strands of pearl cotton, lightweight yarn, or other heavy thread used to add dimension and stability to serged stitches (see page 68).

Floss threaders: Sold as dental-care supplies, these make inexpensive, accessible looper threaders **(R)**.

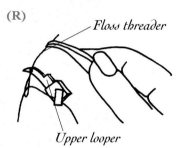

(R)

Floss threader

Upper looper

Foot pedal mat: Vinyl or rubber mat with tiny holes. Used under foot pedal to prevent slipping. Also called "pedal gripper."

Horizontal Thread Holder: Easy-to-use notion that attaches to serger's thread pin to create a horizontal thread rod **(S)**. Horizontal position prevents slippery or wiry thread from falling off cone or spool during serging.

Household needles: Used on some sergers (check manual) and all household sewing machines, they're accessible and available in wide size range and variety of use (ballpoint, stretch, etc.). Labeled 15x1, they feature a flat-sided shank that's inserted toward machine back. See page 84.

(S)

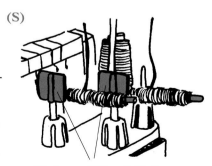

Horizontal Thread Holders

Industrial needles: Used on some sergers (check manual), they're designed to be long-lasting for high-speed sewing (serging). Labeled DCx1, BLx1, DBx1 and JLx1, some feature a rounded shank, some flat. See page 84.

Lint brush: Small brush included with most sergers that cleans inner mechanisms. A stencil or cosmetic brush works well, too.

Looper threader: Long (approximately 6") wire with eye to accommodate any thread (T). Some can be used for needle threading, too. Included with some sergers.

(T) Four different looper threader styles

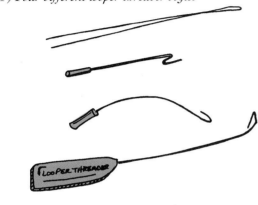

Looper threader in action:

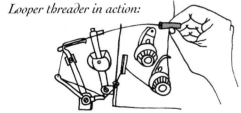

Loop turner: Long, narrow tool with hook on one end. Used to secure thread chain (see "Burying chain tails," page 68).

Monofilament-nylon thread: See pages 85-86.

Needle gripper: Small forceps (often with striated tips) that holds needles for effortless needle insertion, or thread for easy needle threading.

Needle threader/inserter: Handy, inexpensive notion with tiny wire hook at one end for needle threading. A hole in opposite end is for holding needle and inserting its shank into serger's needle clamp (U).

(U) Needle threader/inserter

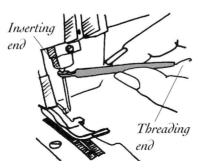

Inserting end

Threading end

Screwdriver: Included with most sergers, it's used for changing feet, needles, and knives (plus stitch settings on some older-model sergers). Long screwdrivers (10"+) are very helpful in loosening hard-to-budge screws.

Seam guide: Adhesive decal with seam-width markings. Adheres to looper cover to gauge serging. Also called "serger guide."

Seam sealant: Liquid sealant, such as Fray Check™, Fray Stop, and No-Fray™, used to secure end of serged stitch (V). Apply to beginning and/or end of serging, let dry, then clip chain tail. Can be removed with rubbing alcohol (test fabric for colorfastness first).

(V)

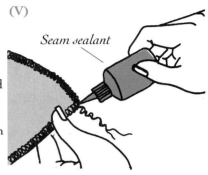

Seam sealant

"Serger" attachment: Foot attachment for sewing machine that trims edge while stitching conventionally. Standard speed and stitch configuration are not altered, but inexpensive and handy if trimming is required. Both generic and name-brand versions are sold (W). Also called a "mini-serger."

(W)

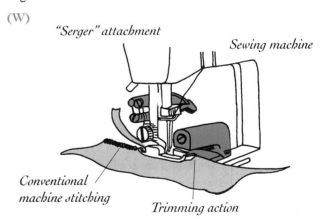

"Serger" attachment

Sewing machine

Conventional machine stitching

Trimming action

Serger labels: Small, adhesive-backed labels used to identify different serger parts/locations (needles, loopers, differential feed, stitch length, stitch width, etc.).

Serger Magic: Cardboard window wheel for recording serger settings (thread type, tension, stitch width, stitch length, differential feed, needle, etc.) for different fabrics.

Serger needles: See "Household needles" (page 74) and "Industrial needles" (above left).

Serger Project Cards: Index-type cards printed in chart form. For recording specific projects and which serger settings (tension, stitch width, stitch length, etc.), thread, and fabric used.

Serger Reference Cards: Index-type cards printed in chart form. For recording serger settings (thread type, tension, stitch width, stitch length, differential feed, needle, attachments, etc.) for different fabrics.

Serger table: Portable, flat, surface that fits against serger's flatbed for larger work surface **(X)**.

(X)

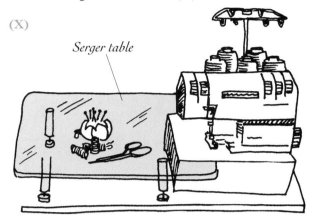

Serger table

Serger thread: See pages 85-87.

Spool cap: Small plastic disc with hole in center. Included with most sergers. When serging with thread spools, place one on spool to ensure even thread feeding and prevent catching on uneven edges or spool notch. Also called "thread unreeling disc" (see page 11).

Spool rings: Small sponge circles placed under cones on thread pins to minimize bouncing and encourage smooth top feeding.

Stabilizing/silencing pads: Used under serger to reduce vibration and noise during serging. (See page 25.)

Surgical seam ripper: Curved instrument featuring surgically sharp blade for easy removal of serged stitches **(Y)**.

(Y)

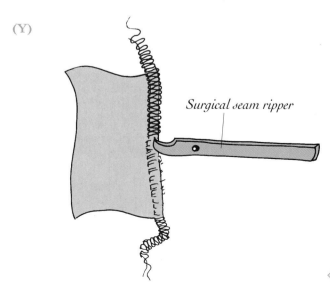

Surgical seam ripper

Tapestry needle: Blunt, large-eyed needle used for burying chain tails.

Thread or trim catchers: Waste bags that catch threads and fabric trimmings during serging. Some are attached to serger front; some are attached to stabilizing pads; and others are independent (included with some sergers) **(Z)**.

(Z)

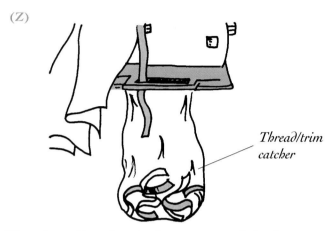

Thread/trim catcher

Thread net: Stretchy, plastic-net, open-ended tubes included with most sergers. Use when serging with slippery threads to prevent thread from slipping off and causing stitch glitches. Also called "spool nets" (see page 11).

Thread Palette: Multiple-spool thread stand that slips onto serger's thread pin. Holds up to five thread spools or cones (decorative and/or all-purpose) for even-feed, hassle-free thread-blending **(Z-1)**.

(Z-1)

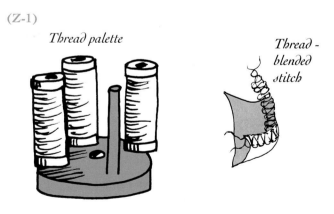

Thread palette

Thread-blended stitch

Vacuum mini-attachments: Small brushes and crevice tools that attach to hose end of most household vacuums for removing lint and dust from serger's hard-to-reach areas.

Water-soluble stabilizer: Thin plastic film, or liquid or spray stabilizer used for producing more uniform, pucker- and tunnel-free serging on limp, slippery, or lightweight fabrics. Washes away for easy removal.

Woolly stretch nylon: See pages 85-86.

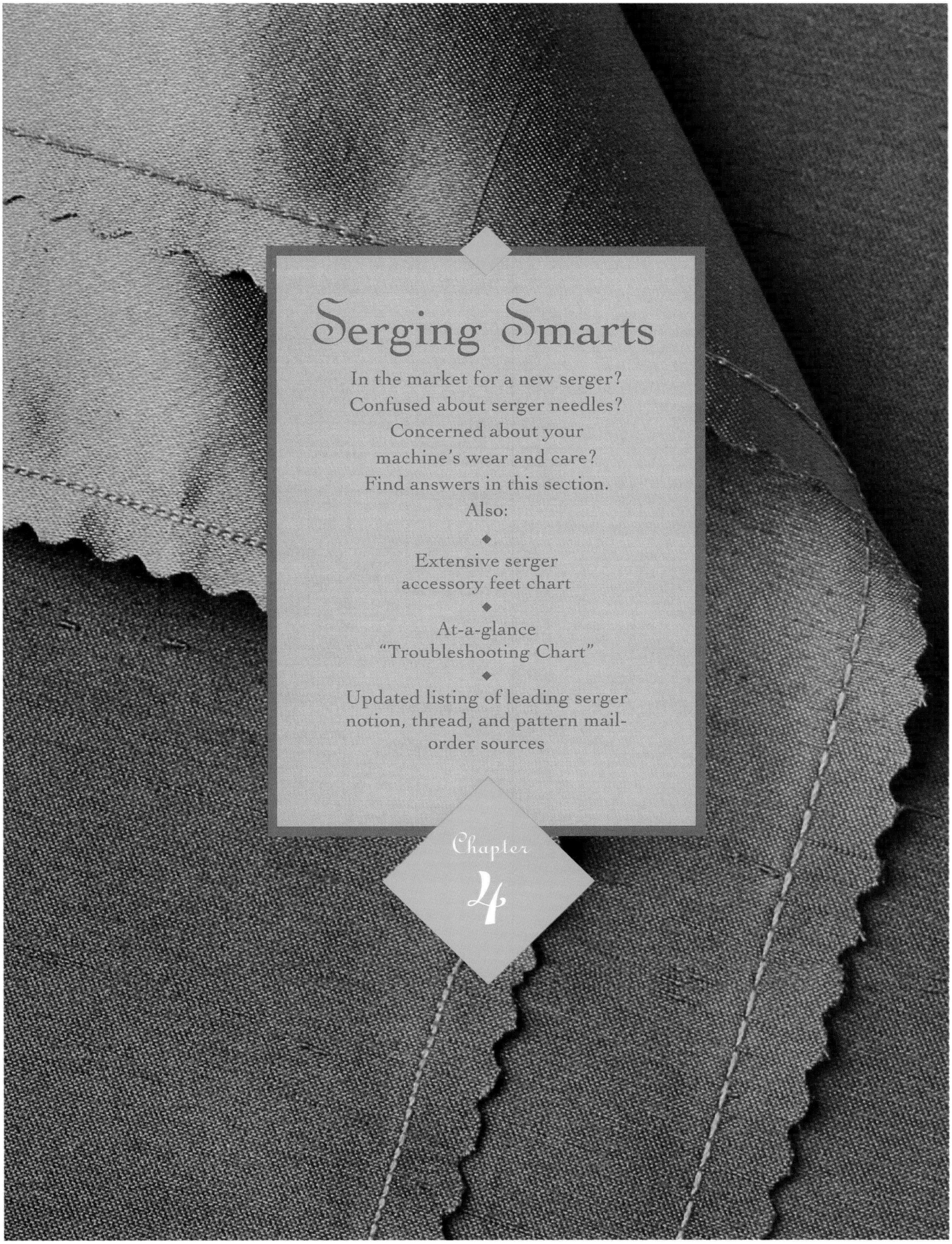

Serging Smarts

In the market for a new serger?
Confused about serger needles?
Concerned about your
machine's wear and care?
Find answers in this section.
Also:

◆

Extensive serger
accessory feet chart

◆

At-a-glance
"Troubleshooting Chart"

◆

Updated listing of leading serger
notion, thread, and pattern mail-
order sources

Chapter

4

Which Serger Should You Buy?

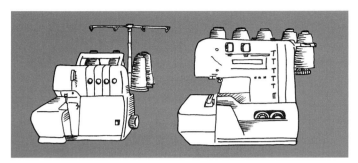

Whether upgrading to a new serger, contemplating adding to your collection or considering your first purchase, take advantage of the following shopping tips and the "Serger Feature Checklist" (page 79). Enjoy prospecting!

◆ **Determine your "serger-user" profile:**

◇ Utilitarian: You occasionally fast-finish and seam, so a basic, no-frills serger might fit the bill.

◇ Creative: You push creativity to the max, experimenting with stitches and the newest decorative threads. Full-featured models should be on your shopping list.

◇ Professional dressmaker or crafter: You sew for business, so focus on sergers that will withstand daily (perhaps rigorous) use, plus offer the stitches and features essential to your work.

◆ **Don't rule out the used market.** If you're a utilitarian serger user, or are on a limited budget, consider used models. Many good, used models are available at very affordable prices. Compare and *always* take for a "test drive."

◆ **Research your shopping options:**

◇ Sewing machine dealers: A good dealer offers advice, new and used sales, repairs and supplies, plus classes and clubs. Look under "Sewing Machines—Household," in the Yellow Pages, or contact the machine companies featured in "Insider Insights" (page 54), for dealer referrals.

◇ Fabric stores and departments: Service and models offered vary greatly, depending on the personnel's enthusiasm for serger sales and education. Increasingly, fabric chain stores are offering sergers. In some areas, they're the only retail option.

◇ Mass-merchandisers: Penney's, Sears, Spiegel, and others sell and sometimes rebrand sergers for sale in stores and catalogs. While "self-service," they're attractive due to competitive pricing on affordable models, revolving credit plans, and accessibility in areas void of dealerships.

◇ Discount retailers: CostCo, Price Club, Wal-Mart, and others offer enticing prices. This self-serve option is best for those comfortable learning and maintaining on their own. Warranties may be valid only by shipping back to the manufacturer for repairs.

◇ Mail-order specialists: Convenience and selection are pluses. Clarify return, warranty, and service policies before buying with a major credit card. Also, be sure your source is an authorized dealer for the brands being offered (if not, the warranty may be invalid).

◇ Classified ads, estate and garage sales: For these as-is sergers, prices run from rock-bottom to inflated. Recommended only for experienced serger seamsters, or those advised by a helpful dealer or knowledgeable friend.

◆ **Take any prospective serger for a "test drive."** Conscientious dealers and retailers encourage test-serging, preferably during nonpeak store hours. For the most valid testing, bring samples of your favorite fabrics and threads. When test-serging is not an option, be sure to buy with a return guarantee.

◆ **Don't let price be your only criterion.** It may be wiser to pay more for a serger sold by a reliable, service-oriented dealer. (You will rarely pay list price, no matter where you shop.) Inquire about their grace period for upgrades, so you can trade up your model for the difference in price.

◆ **Ask questions about repairs.** Find out where repairs are done. If shipping is required, determine whether you're responsible for the charges. Normal turnaround time? Cost of yearly maintenance?

◆ **Compare models and brands.** Photocopy the "Serger Feature Checklist" (page 79), and fill in for each model considered. Narrow down to those models with the features you covet, then compare.

Serger Feature Checklist*

Serger brand/model_____

Location_____

Stitch options available? (See pages 66-67.)
__2-thread overedging (flatlocking, wrapped/seam)?
__2-thread chainstitching?
__3-thread overlocking (flatlocking, wrapped/seam)?
__3-thread cover hemming/stitching?
__4-thread overlocking?
__4-thread safety stitching?
__4-thread mock safety stitching?
__5-thread overlocking?

__ **Narrow-rolled edging option?** (See pages 42-43, 66-67)
__Easily adjusted without changing plates or feet?
__2-thread and/or __3-thread narrow-rolled edge?

__ **Variable stitch width? If so, range:**_____.
(See pages 20-21, 22-23, 73.)
__Width easily changed without tools, plates, or feet?

__ **Stitch length easily adjusted?** Range:_____.
__ Length easily changed without tools?
__Adjustment external for easy accessibility

__ **Differential feed? If so, range:**_____.
(See pages 38, 69.)__Easy to reach and use?

__ **Easy to thread?** Circle: Self-threading lower looper
and/or looper(s), needle threader?
__Accommodates decorative threads?

__ **Easy tension adjustments for various thread/fabric types?**
Lay-in/inset_____Beehive/dial_____

__ **Tension-release capability?** (See page 73.)

__ **Easy-to-change feet?** Snap-on ___ shank ___.
(See pages 80-83.)

__ **Adjustable presser foot pressure?** (See page 70.)

__ **Built-in light?**

__ **Moderate noise and vibration?**

__ **Upper knife disengageable without tools?**
(See pages 32-33, 70)

__ **Variable serging speed?** SPM:_____ (See page 72.)

__ **Knee-lift presser foot option?** (See page 72.)

__ **LED or LCD panel display for stitch settings?**
(See pages 70, 72.)

__ **Safety helps?** Circle: Finger guard, off/on switch,
auto-shut-off?

__ **Needle type?** Circle: Household, industrial?
(See pages 74-75, 84.)

__ **Separate set-screw for each needle?** (See page 72.)

__ **Standard accessories?** Circle: Tweezers, spool caps, thread
nets, screwdriver(s), extra needles, looper threader, knife
blade, oil, needle inserter, rolled-edge foot/plate?

__ **Optional accessories?** Circle: trim catcher, seam-width
guide, carrying bag?
Others_____.

__ **Feet?** (See pages 80-83.) Circle: blind hem, elastic-
application, cording or gimp, cover hem, ribbon tape or
trim, piping, beading (pearl/sequin), shirring, binding,
lace-application?

__ **Limited warranty?**_____years. Items covered?

__ **Confidence in the dealer's service and knowledge?**
Circle: Introductory classes, introductory video,
introductory workbook, ongoing serger classes/clubs?

__ **Repair services, annual checkups, parts readily available?**

__ **Upgrade path option available?** Time period?
____months

__ **Do you like the "feel" and look of the serger?**

* Photocopy this checklist; fill out one for each model being
considered.

Serge with Your Feet

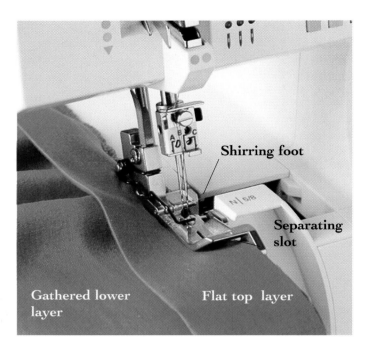

Shirring foot

Separating slot

Gathered lower layer

Flat top layer

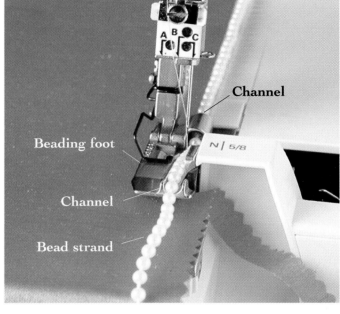

Channel

Beading foot

Channel

Bead strand

Saving time, ensuring accuracy, preventing undue wear, and multiplying creative possibilities. These are just some of the many reasons seamsters are intrigued with serger feet. Yet the wide range of types and prices can be a bit daunting to those new to "serging with your feet."

To provide an overview of feet compatibility, availability, and applicability before you buy, we've compiled these tips and a comprehensive chart for all brands:

◆ When shopping for a new or used serger, don't forget about feet. Ask which feet are standard (included in the price) and which are optional. Also ask if there are other generic or brand-name feet that will work with the prospective model.

◆ Be aware that all the feet shown on pages 81-83 are not compatible with, or available for, all models. Foot configuration may vary brand to brand, or even model to model, but applications will be similar.

◆ To avoid incompatibility problems, know your serger brand and model number. Feet are usually not interchangeable among brands, or even among models within a brand. And generic feet aren't necessarily compatible with all sergers.

◆ Determine whether your serger has shank-style or snap-on feet, and buy accordingly. Inquire

about adapters if you're interested in snap-on feet for your shank-style model.

◆ If sticking to a budget is crucial, study "Applications" on the chart, then decide if one or two additional feet would suffice. For instance, a beading foot can help apply wire, bead strands, sequins, filler cord, and cording.

◆ If you can't find optional feet in your area, consider mail-order sources (see pages 91-92).

◆ Compare prices, but don't buy on price alone. A foot that doesn't function dependably—or worse yet, damages your serger—is not a good value.

◆ Whether buying from a local store, or by mail-order, *always buy with a return guarantee.*

◆ Test-serge with care. First, read the instructions. Fasten the new foot (don't use it if it doesn't fit or is hard to attach). Check the needle position; only the right or left needle position can be used with certain feet. Finally, advance the stitch by hand. A stitch should form smoothly and quietly.

◆ Play with your feet, devising new ways to expand the functional and creative capabilities of your serger.

Serger Feet/Accessories Chart

Foot/Attachment	Description	Applications
Beading, Pearl, or Pearl/Sequin Foot 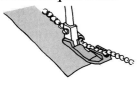	Front and back channels guide dimensional strands between the needle and knives, directly under the stitch.	◆ Applying pearl strands ◆ Applying sequin strands ◆ Applying cording/filler ◆ Applying fishing line ◆ Applying wire
Bias Binder Attachment 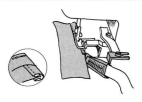	Folds flat bias fabric strip over the edge so that it can be secured with serged chainstitching.	◆ Applying flat bias fabric strip to edge as binding. *Must be used with serged chainstitching*
Bias Tape Guide/ Piping Attachment 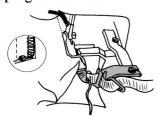	Folds bias strip over filler cord to make piping. Can also make piping or bias strip insert while serging in a seam or to an edge.	◆ Making piping ◆ Making and inserting piping in a serged seam ◆ Making bias insert in a serged seam
Blind Hem Foot 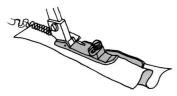	Guides fabric to the right of the needle, varying the needleline position and trimming width (if any).	◆ Serged blind hemming ◆ Even-width flatlocking ◆ Even-width trimming ◆ Even-width fagoting ◆ Even, no-trim serging
Cording Foot 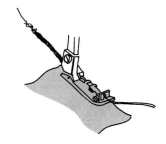	Guides cording through a hole and/or channel in the foot, directly under the stitch. Cording diameter capacity varies.	◆ Applying cording ◆ Applying fine wire ◆ Applying fine fishing line
Cover Hem/Stitch: Belt Loop Foot 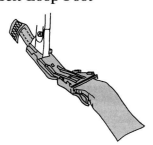	Slot in front of foot folds under long edges of 1" bias strip, securing the edges with cover hem stitching.	◆ Making belt loops ◆ Making narrow straps ◆ Applying bias strips to another piece of fabric

Foot/Attachment	Description	Applications
Cover Hem/Stitch: Cover Hem Foot & 1" Cover Hem Guide 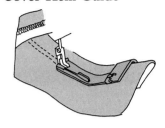	Slot in the clear foot attachment folds under a 1"-wide hem, securing it with cover stitching. Must be used with cover hem foot and cover hem/stitch.	◆ 1"-deep cover hem stitch
Cover Hem/Stitch: Cover Hem Foot & Wrapped Seam Guide 	Slots in clear foot attachment wrap the tape over edge, securing it with cover hem stitching. Must be used with cover hem foot and cover hem/stitch.	◆ Applying wide bias tape or extra-wide double-fold bias tape to an edge
Elastic Foot or "Elasticator" 	An adjustment screw on the front of the foot regulates the amount of elastic stretch while it is being applied.	◆ Applying narrow elastic ◆ Applying narrow trim ◆ Applying narrow ribbon
Gimp Foot or Cording Foot 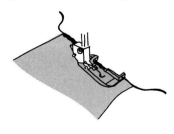	Guides fine gimp through a hole and/or channel in the foot, directly under the stitch.	◆ Applying fine gimp ◆ Applying very fine wire ◆ Applying fine fishing line ◆ Applying fine cording
Heirloom Serging or Lace Foot 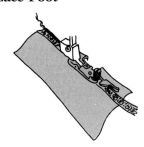	Front-edge guide aligns the fabric for ultra-narrow seaming or finishing.	◆ Finishing lace trim ◆ Inserting lace trim ◆ Narrow seaming ◆ Narrow pintucking

Foot/Attachment	Description	Applications
Multipurpose Foot 	Specialty foot that integrates features of beading and piping feet. Can use with gathering attachment.	◆ Applying beads, sequins, or pearls ◆ Applying zippers ◆ Making/applying piping ◆ Combining with gathering attachment features
Narrow-Rolled Hem Foot 	A narrower, sometimes shorter, stitch finger creates a narrower stitch. Some models do not require changing the foot (or plate) for narrow-rolled hemming.	◆ Narrow-rolled hemming and seaming ◆ Narrow balanced-tension finishing and seaming ◆ Narrow flatlocking ◆ Narrow pintucking
Piping Foot 	A groove on the underside of the foot accommodates piping cording for smooth, even serging.	◆ Inserting piping in seam ◆ Making piping ◆ Serging zippers (position teeth in the groove)
Ribbon/Tape Foot 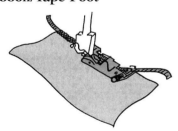	Path or hole in front of the foot guides ribbon or tape directly under stitch. May be part of standard foot.	◆ Applying narrow ribbon ◆ Applying narrow trim ◆ Applying narrow cloth tape
Separator Attachment/Fabric Separator, or Gathering/Attachment 	Slot in front of foot separates and keeps the top layer flat, while gathering the lower layer. Use with "plus" differential feed.	◆ Gathering ruffles while seaming to flat fabric ◆ Gathering one section while seaming to another ◆ Gathering single-layer ◆ Combining gathering with other specialty feet applications
Transparent Chainstitch Foot 	Clear, shorter (than standard) foot allows viewing the stitch while serging. Use with chainstitch.	◆ Straight chainstitching ◆ Fine-tuning chainstitch tensions ◆ Shirring fabric with elastic thread in looper

Needle Know-How

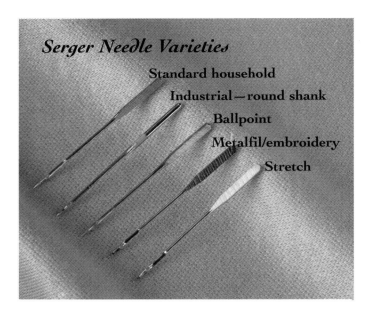

Serger Needle Varieties

Standard household
Industrial—round shank
Ballpoint
Metalfil/embroidery
Stretch

Needles are crucial to serging because they secure the looper threads. If the needle thread is pulled out, the stitch falls apart. Also, the needle type, condition, position and threading method must work in unison with the loopers; if any one factor is out of sync, no stitch is formed, or the stitch is irregular.

Knowing needles—which types and sizes to use, when to change them (page 90), how to insert and remove them (pages 28-29)—is easier than you might imagine. You'll soon recognize needle-caused problems and their solutions. Some tips:

◆ Make note of the needle type recommended for your serger model. If your manual is misplaced, study your machine—correct sizes and types are usually printed or stamped somewhere on the casing (often inside the looper cover). Write down the number, and keep in your wallet for reference.

◆ Differentiate between needle types:

✧ **Industrial needles:** Can be round-or flat-shanked, commonly sized 11/80 or 14/90. Varieties include DCx1, BLx1, DBxl, and JLx1, in both sharp and ballpoint (use the specific type required for your serger). Stronger and slightly shorter than household needles, industrial needles can be more difficult to locate in stores. And the round-shank versions tend to be more difficult to align correctly in the needle clamp.

✧ **Household needles:** Flat-shanked (available in both sharp and ballpoint varieties) are sold in the full range of sizes, from 8/60 to 19/120. However, the recommended size range for sergers is 9/70 to 14/90. Smaller sizes can't withstand the speed and rigors of serging. Some larger sizes won't fit into a serger, can throw off the timing, or worse yet, damage a looper.

✧ **Specialty needles:** Household needles engineered to solve stitching problems:

Schmetz ELx705 help prevent skipped stitches.

Organ brand HAX1SP are Japanese-made needles that also prevent skipped stitches, and are recommended specifically for 534, 534D, 200-series, and 734 White Superlocks.

Stretch needles have rounded tips and deeper scarves to solve skipped stitches on knits, elastics.

Metalfil, Schmetz Embroidery, and topstitching needles minimize thread breakage and fraying.

Microtex/Sharp needles are designed by Schmetz for sewing and serging microfibers.

◆ On multiple-needle models, use the same brand, type, and size throughout. Exception: Some early models required a different needle type in each position—check your manual.

◆ Always have extra needles on hand. Murphy's law prevails: With a deadline pending and all stores closed, you will break your last needle.

◆ Insert/position needles properly (see pages 28-29).

◆ Recognize potential needle-related problems: no stitch formation or irregular stitches (pages 10-11); skipped stitches (pages 18-19); chainstitch won't form (page 24); clicking or excessive noise (page 25); and runs and holes in the fabric (page 31). Any or all may be symptomatic of a damaged or misaligned needle.

◆ Note that needles dull faster when serging on synthetic fabrics, especially polyesters, batting, fake furs, metallics, and microfibers. Inspect needles closely after serging any of these fabrics.

Thread Pictorial

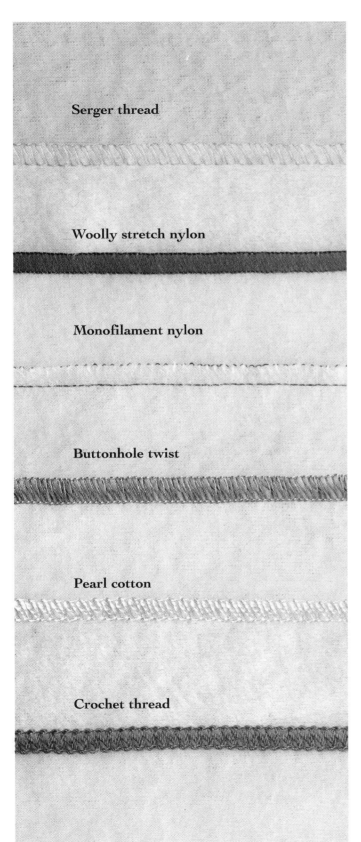

Serger thread

Woolly stretch nylon

Monofilament nylon

Buttonhole twist

Pearl cotton

Crochet thread

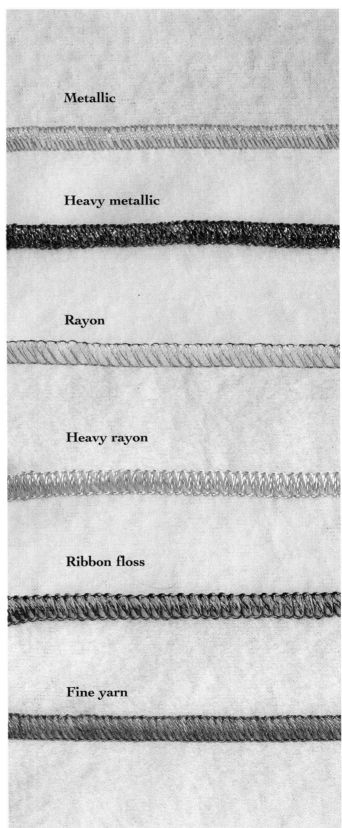

Metallic

Heavy metallic

Rayon

Heavy rayon

Ribbon floss

Fine yarn

Thread Chart

	Serger Thread	All-Purpose Thread	Mono-filament Nylon	Woolly Stretch Nylon	Button-hole Twist	Pearl Cotton	Crochet Thread
General Uses	Finish Seam Flatlock Rolled edge Chainstitch Cover stitch	Finish Seam Flatlock Rolled edge Chainstitch Cover stitch	Finish Seam Flatlock** Rolled edge Chainstitch —	Finish Seam Flatlock Rolled edge Chainstitch Cover stitch	Finish Seam Flatlock Rolled edge Chainstitch Cover stitch	Finish Seam Flatlock Rolled edge Chainstitch Cover stitch	Finish Seam Flatlock Rolled edge Chainstitch Cover stitch
Ease of Use	Easy	Easy	Easy	Easy	Easy	Moderate-Challenging	Moderate-Challenging
Where to Use	Needle Looper(s)	Needle Looper(s)	Needle Looper(s)	Needle Looper(s)	Needle Looper(s)	— Looper(s)	— Looper(s)
Tension(s)	Normal	Normal	Loosen	Loosen a lot	Loosen	Loosen	Loosena
Stitch Length	Medium	Medium	Shorten	Shorten	Shorten	Lengthen	Lengthen
Stitch Width	Medium	Medium	Medium	Widen	Narrow Slightly	Widen	Widen
Availability*	A, B, C	A, B, C	A, B, C	A, B, C	A, B	A, B, C	A, B

* A = widely available (fabric/craft stores, sewing machine dealerships); B = mail-order thread catalogs; C = mail-order notions catalogs (see "Serger Notions and Threads by Mail," pages 91–92)

Flatlock over ribbon, cord or other trim. ***Note:* Uses and settings may vary with serger model, fabric type and weight, etc.

Serger thread: Lighter-weight (than all-purpose) thread cross-wound onto cones or tubes for easy, even feeding during high-speed serging. Many brands (see page 85).

All-purpose thread: Standard-weight thread parallel-wound onto thread spools. Many brands.

Monofilament-nylon: Strong, "invisible" thread in clear or smoke tone. Flexible, lighter weights work best: YLI Miracle Nylon Monofilament Thread, Sulky Premium Invisible, Wonder Thread (in different weights), and other brands (see page 85).

Woolly stretch nylon: Strong, soft, stretchy, crimped, untwisted nylon thread that spreads over the edge. Available in wide range of solids, plus variegated colors, metallics, and a heavier-weight variety, Woolly Nylon Extra (YLI). J & P Coats Bulky Lock, YLI Woolly Nylon and other brands (see pages 69, 71, 85).

Buttonhole twist: Highly twisted, cordlike thread. Also called topstitching or buttonhole thread. Sold in wide color range. J & P Coats Dual Duty Plus®, Kanagawa Silk Stitch, YLI Jeans Stitch, and other brands (see pages 46, 85).

Pearl cotton: Mercerized all-cotton thread that's soft, shiny and not highly twisted. Available in wide color range, including variegated hues, on balls, skeins, or cones. DMC No. 5 (finer) and 8 Pearl Cotton, J & P Coats No. 5 Pearl Cotton, and other brands (see pages 69, 85).

Crochet thread: Strong, highly twisted cotton or acrylic thread. Available in wide color range, and wound onto balls. J & P Coats Knit-Cro-Sheen and other brands (see pages 69, 85).

	Metallic Thread	Heavy Metallic Thread	Rayon Thread	Heavy Rayon Thread	Silk Thread	Ribbon/ Ribbon Floss	Fine Yarn
General Uses	Finish Seam Flatlock Rolled edge Chainstitch Cover stitch	Finish Seam Flatlock Rolled edge Chainstitch Cover stitch	Finish Seam Flatlock Rolled edge Chainstitch Cover stitch	Finish Seam Flatlock Rolled edge Chainstitch Cover stitch	Finish Seam Flatlock Rolled edge Chainstitch Cover stitch	Finish — Flatlock — Chainstitch Cover stitch	Finish — Flatlock — Chainstitch Cover stitch
Ease of Use	Moderate	Moderate	Easy	Moderate	Easy	Moderate-Challenging	Moderate-Challenging
Where to Use	Needle Looper(s)	— Looper(s)	Needle Looper(s)	— Looper(s)	— Looper(s)	— Looper(s)	— Looper(s)
Tension(s)	Loosen A Lot	Loosen Slightly	Tighten Slightly	Loosen Slightly	Normal-Tighten Slightly	Loosen	Loosen
Stitch Length	Shorten	Lengthen	Shorten	Lengthen	Shorten	Lengthen	Lengthen
Stitch Width	Narrow Slightly	Widen	Medium	Widen	Medium	Widen	Medium
Availability*	A, B, C	B, C	A, B, C	B, C	A, B, C	B, C	A, B, C

Metallic thread: Fine to all-purpose weight threads that produce sparkling edge finishes. Gutermann Metallic, J & P Coats Metallic, Madeira Supertwist, Sulky Sliver Metallic Thread™, and other brands (see pages 69, 85).

Heavy metallic thread/yarn: Lofty metallics that offer great coverage and shine. Madeira Glamour, YLI Candlelight, and other brands (see pages 46, 69, 85).

Rayon thread: Shiny machine embroidery thread available in wide and brilliant color range. Madeira 30-Weight Rayon, Sulky Embroidery Thread, YLI Ultrasheen™ rayon-like acrylic, and other brands (see pages 46, 69, 71, 85).

Heavy rayon thread: Lofty, shiny threads that produce a beautiful, lustrous finish. Available in wide color range. Some are untwisted for extra sheen, but are less durable than those twisted.

Madeira Decor 6 (untwisted), YLI Pearl Crown Rayon (twisted), YLI Designer 6 (slightly twisted) (see pages 69, 85).

Silk thread: Shiny, strong thread in broad color range and variety of weights. Kanagawa Silk Embroidery Thread, TIRE Line Stitch, and other brands (see page 46).

Ribbon/ribbon floss: Soft, lightweight, in narrow widths (⅟₁₆″ to ¼″), both woven and braided (floss). A wide color range in acrylic, cotton, rayon, and silk (polyester and nylon are usually too stiff). Woven and softer, braided varieties. Kanagawa Silk (woven), Ribbon Floss™ (braided), and Ribbon Thread™ (braided) (see pages 46, 69, 85).

Yarn: Fine, strong, tightly twisted yarns, such as machine-knitting or needlepunch machine yarn, work best. Clarke's Oh Sew Easy, Plaid's Purr-Fect Punch®, Success® (see pages 46, 69, 85).

Troubleshooting Chart

Can't Balance Tensions
(pages 8-9)

- Turn knobs right to tighten, left to loosen.
- Turn lay-in dials up to tighten, down to loosen.
- Tighten loopy threads, or to hide threads.
- Loosen puckered threads, or to expose more thread.
- Loosen tightest tension first.
- Shorten or narrow to loosen tension.
- Lengthen or widen to tighten tension.
- Loosen for heavier thread or fabric.

No Stitch Formation
(pages 10, 48-49)

- Check threading paths.
- Confirm needles are fully inserted.
- Be sure needle type and size are correct.
- Position needles properly.
- Lower presser foot.
- Place all threads under presser foot and gently pull tails to advance stitch.

Irregular Stitch Formation
(pages 11, 48-49)

- Check threading paths.
- Balance tensions.
- Replace needle and position properly.
- Be sure thread is feeding smoothly.
- Lengthen stitch slightly.
- Tighten tensions slightly: loopers first, then, if necessary, the needle.

Can't (or Afraid to) Rethread
(page 12)

- If serger is already threaded, use tie-on threading method.
- If serger is unthreaded, look up the manual threading guide and sequence.
- Use serger tweezers, looper and needle threaders for guides, loopers, and eyes.
- Follow color-coded guides on machine and/or manual.

Can't Convert from a 3-Thread to 2-Thread, and Back
(page 13)

- Make sure model will convert to 2-thread.
- Determine 2-thread configuration; 2/4- and 2-thread models require no conversion.
- Clip upper looper thread (below tension dial).
- Refer to conversion steps in manual or on inside of looper casing.
- Activate converter for 2-thread serging; deactivate to return to 3-thread serging.

Thread Breakage
(pages 14-15)

- Loosen tensions one at a time, starting with thread that breaks most frequently.
- Rethread from scratch, following manual's and/or dealer's recommendation for sequence.
- Rethread needle after threading loopers, or draw up needle thread above throat plate after rethreading.
- Change to a new and/or specialty needle.
- Test for burrs on looper tips and eyes.

Hairy Edges
(pages 16-17)

- Trim edge at least slightly.
- Shorten stitch length.
- Change to thicker or multifilament thread.
- Reposition or replace lower knife.
- Serge over edge twice.
- Serge over layer of water-soluble stabilizer.
- For rolled edges, increase stitch width or bite.
- Apply seam sealant to trimming line.

Skipped Stitches
(pages 18-19)

- Visually trace threading paths for accuracy.
- Change to a new needle.
- For knits, use stretch or ballpoint needle.
- Try a new, different size needle.
- Loosen the tightest tension.
- Watch for label glue on spool or cone.
- Prewash fabric to remove finishes.
- Increase foot pressure.

Stitch Isn't Wide Enough
(pages 20-21)

- Widen stitch width or bite.
- Use left needle of 3/4-thread stitch.
- Use correct foot and/or plate.
- Loosen looper tensions.
- Shorten stitch length.
- Change to thicker looper thread.
- Recheck threading, especially loopers.

Stitch Isn't Narrow Enough
(pages 22-23)

- Narrow stitch width or bite.
- Use right needle of 3/4-thread stitch.
- Use correct foot and/or plate.
- Rethread loopers with finer thread.
- Adjust for rolled edge (use rolled or balanced-tension settings).
- Tighten looper tensions.
- Use softer and/or thinner fabric.

Chainstitch Won't Form, or Breaks
(page 24)

- Insert chainstitch needle properly.
- Balance chainstitch tensions.
- Be sure chainstitch needle and looper guides and eyes are threaded properly.
- Loosen needle tension.
- Lengthen stitch to at least 2.5mm.
- Start chainstitching on fabric, not "air."
- Replace needle if damaged.

Clicking, Excessive Noise
(page 25)

- Visually trace threading paths.
- For clicking noise, replace needle. If clicking doesn't stop, consult dealer.
- Properly align upper and lower knife blades.
- Replace needle with new and possibly smaller size one.
- Loosen tightest tensions.
- Clean and oil serger.

Machine Jams
(pages 26-27)

- Stop! Don't continue serging.
- Cut away thread or fabric wrapped around stitch finger and/or looper(s).
- To prevent, serge with looper cover closed.
- If needle is up, remove foot and disengage knives; remove/cut off of stitch finger.
- If needle is down, raise needle bar, remove foot, and remove/cut off jams.

Can't Remove or Insert Needles Properly
(pages 28-29)

- Consult manual.
- Use recommended needle type and size.
- Raise needle to highest position.
- Loosen correct set-screw(s).
- If there's only one set-screw, remove or replace both needles together.
- Grip with special tweezers or grippers.
- Align needle correctly.

Copyright © 1996 by Naomi Baker, Gail Brown, Cindy Kacynski:
The Ultimate Serger Answer Guide. Reprint by permission only.

Needle Breakage
(page 30)
- Insert new needle, correctly.
- Change to larger needle.
- Loosen needle and upper looper tensions.
- Visually trace threading paths to needle.
- Don't tug on fabric or thread chain.
- Don't pull/serge thread knots through eyes.

Pulled Threads, Runs and/or Holes in Fabric
(page 31)
- Replace needle.
- Change to a smaller, ballpoint and/or stretch needle.
- Use a finer or softer thread.
- Lengthen the stitch.
- Loosen the needle tension.
- Fold under ⅜" hem, and serge without trimming.

Edges are Ragged or Not Cut At All
(pages 32-33)
- Engage upper knife.
- Move fabric to right to allow for trimming.
- Move fabric to left to trim less, or pretrim.
- Reset lower knife.
- If fabric is too thick, compress with zigzagging, or pretrim.
- If fabric is heavy, lock upper knife.
- Clean and lubricate knives.
- Replace worn blades.

Puckers
(pages 34-35)
- Loosen needle tension.
- Visually trace threading paths for tangled or trapped threads.
- Watch for label glue on spool or cone.
- Shorten stitch length.
- Adjust for minus differential feeding.
- Taut-serge.
- Use finer thread and smaller needle.

Excessive Stretching
(pages 36-37)
- Lengthen stitch.
- Trim at least ¼" while serging.
- Adjust for plus differential feeding.
- Ease-plus while serging.
- Adjust for lighter presser foot pressure.
- Don't stretch edge while serging.
- Use finer thread.
- Serge over filler or through elastic.

Differential Feed Isn't Working
(page 38)
For gathering and stretch control:
- Adjust for plus-setting.
- Lengthen stitch.
- Use softer, lighter fabric or single layer.
- Ease-plus.
- Tighten needle tension.

For puckering:
- Adjust for minus-setting
- Shorten stitch.
- Use heavier, stiffer fabric, or add layers.
- Taut-serge.
- Loosen needle tension.

Seam Spreads Open and/or Unravels
(page 39)
For spreading seams:
- Tighten needle tension.
- Use stretch thread in needle.
- Change from 2-thread to 3- or 3/4-thread stitch.
- Use knit rather than woven fabric.

For unraveling seams or edges:
- Finish with seam sealant and trim tails.
- Bury tails of heavier threads.
- Serge over thread chain.

Can't Determine a Seam Edge or Position
(page 40)
- Mark needle (seamline) positions on foot front.
- Test to determine correct seam width.
- Mark start seam allowances on looper cover, or purchase adhesive seamline guides.
- Skim, don't trim edges when serge-finishing before seaming.
- Allow wider (1") allowances if seaming after serge-finishing.

Ugly Curves and Corners
(page 41)
For curves:
- Practice on scraps, watching knife.
- Serge slowly and consistently.
- Narrow width if stitch tunnels.
- Trim while serging.
- Adjust for plus differential feeding when needed.

For corners:
- Serge off, then serge adjacent edge.
- Round slightly.
- Finish fine threads with seam sealant.
- Finish heavier threads by burying tail.

Rolled Edge Snafus
(pages 42-43)
- Widen stitch width or bite.
- Use narrow stitch finger.
- Shorten stitch length.
- Properly adjust tensions for narrow rolled edge.
- Use woolly stretch nylon or fine monofilament-nylon in 2-thread needle or 3-thread lower looper.
- For heavy fabrics, change to wrapped stitch.

Faulty Flatlocking
(pages 44-45)
- Properly adjust tensions for flatlocking.
- Allow stitches to hang off fold or edge.
- Use correct threads in proper locations.
- Use spongy, ravel-free knits.
- Serge an even width from fold, or trim fabric edge while serging.
- Shorten stitch length and/or use heavier thread to prevent hairy edges.

Edge Won't Lettuce
(page 51)
- Use fabric that stretches.
- Adjust for minus differential feeding.
- Taut-serge.
- Shorten stitch length.

Seams Pop in Stretch Fabric
(page 52)
- Loosen needle tension slightly.
- Use woolly stretch nylon in needle.
- Use polyester or polyester-blend thread.

Thread Shreds During Serging
(page 52)
- Use high-quality thread.
- Replace needle.
- Use needle one size larger and/or topstitching or specialty needle.
- Blend with stronger thread.

Stitches Bunch Up During Elastic Application
(page 52)
- Adjust for longest stitch length.
- Anchor stitches in elastic extension.
- Stretch elastic in front of and behind foot.

Copyright© 1996 by Naomi Baker, Gail Brown, Cindy Kacynski: *The Ultimate Serger Answer Guide.* **Reprint by permission only.**

How-to's for Healthy Sergers

Before you begin:

Read your manual—most explain maintenance quite thoroughly. Also, if possible, solicit your dealer's recommendations for care and servicing.

Annual checkup:

Treat your machine to a once-a-year professional (dealer) cleaning and tune-up. You'll gain improved serging performance and a longer machine life. While there, stock up on oil, cleaning tools, spare needles, knives, and lights.

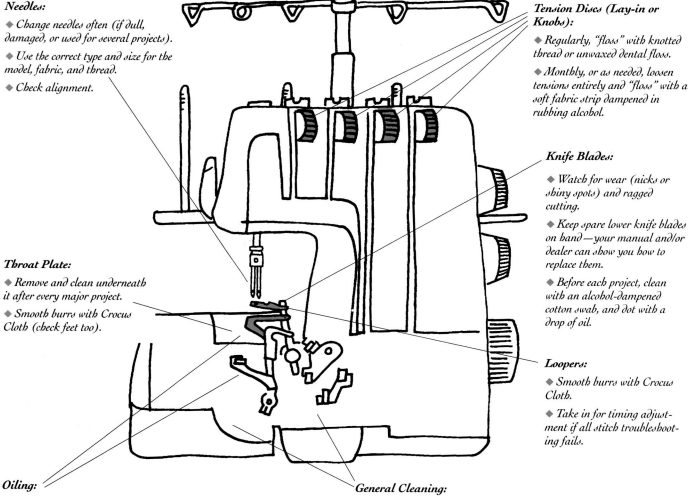

Needles:

◆ *Change needles often (if dull, damaged, or used for several projects).*

◆ *Use the correct type and size for the model, fabric, and thread.*

◆ *Check alignment.*

Throat Plate:

◆ *Remove and clean underneath it after every major project.*

◆ *Smooth burrs with Crocus Cloth (check feet too).*

Oiling:

◆ *Clean before oiling.*

◆ *Use only sewing machine oil.*

◆ *Check manual for lubrication locations (where metal parts are moving or rubbing together) and frequency (about every 8 hours of serging, or after each major project).*

◆ *Lightly oil, removing excess with a fabric scrap.*

◆ *Oil if running noisily even when unthreaded.*

◆ *Do not oil if self-lubricating. Run unthreaded, warming up metal to release lubrication. If not used for several weeks, may need oiling; check with your dealer.*

Tension Discs (Lay-in or Knobs):

◆ *Regularly, "floss" with knotted thread or unwaxed dental floss.*

◆ *Monthly, or as needed, loosen tensions entirely and "floss" with a soft fabric strip dampened in rubbing alcohol.*

Knife Blades:

◆ *Watch for wear (nicks or shiny spots) and ragged cutting.*

◆ *Keep spare lower knife blades on hand—your manual and/or dealer can show you how to replace them.*

◆ *Before each project, clean with an alcohol-dampened cotton swab, and dot with a drop of oil.*

Loopers:

◆ *Smooth burrs with Crocus Cloth.*

◆ *Take in for timing adjustment if all stitch troubleshooting fails.*

General Cleaning:

◆ *Use oil-dampened lint, makeup, or stencil brush to remove heavy lint.*

◆ *Use miniature vacuum cleaners, hair dryers (on cool setting), or environmentally safe, moisture-free canned air to remove light lint.*

◆ *Don't blow lint into inaccessible areas.*

◆ *Check for lint inside casing, between knives, under throat plate.*

◆ *Clean and dust outer casing with rubbing alcohol.*

◆ *As needed, unscrew the underside casing and wash the casing in soap and water.*

Serging Notions and Threads by Mail

Shop your local fabric stores and sewing machine dealers for notions and threads—both utilitarian and decorative. Our guess is that you'll be surprised by the selections available and welcome the opportunity to buy notions, colors, and textures that are ready to serge today.

Remember, too, that when time is short, driving is too far, or in-store shopping is just plain impossible, most dealers and many stores will gladly ship credit-card and C.O.D. orders.

When you're unable to find certain items, look to these established mail-order companies for most, if not all, of the serger threads and notions referenced in this book. (There are many more mail-order suppliers to recommend, but we've focused on specialists in mail-order and serging supplies.) For additional sources, refer to mail-order advertisements in national sewing publications.

Let us know if we've missed your favorite serger-supply source (see page 96). Also, please alert us of unreliable service, substandard products, or questionable pricing policies.

All-Brand Discount Sew & Serg, 9789 Florida Boulevard, Baton Rouge, LA 70815, phone (800) SEW-SERG, fax (800) 866-1261, e-mail sewserg@aol.com, web site www.allbrands.com. Call or send SASE for information. Generic and branded serger accessory feet, serger notions, books, and furniture.

Atlanta Thread & Supply Co., 695 Red Oak Road, Stockbridge, GA 30281, phone (800) 847-1001, fax (800) 298-0403. All types of serger threads, notions, and supplies. Free catalog.

Banasch's, 2810 Highland Avenue, Cincinnati, OH 45212, phone (800) 543-0355 or (513) 731-2040, fax (513) 731-2090. Great selection of coned threads, serger needles, thread stands, knives, and more. Free catalog.

Clotilde Inc., B3000, Louisiana, MO 63353, phone (800) 772-2891, fax (800) 863-3191, e-mail clotilde@clotilde.com, web site www.clotilde.com. Various threads (decorative, serger, monofilament-nylon), serger videos, serger notions. Free catalog.

Home-Sew, Box 4099, Dept. BOK, Bethlehem, PA 18018, phone (800) 344-4739, fax (610) 867-9717. Some serger notions, plus affordably priced coned polyester and monofilament threads and elastics. Free catalog.

Linda Lee Originals, 2480 Riniel Road, Lennon, MI 48449, phone (810) 621-4665, fax (810) 621-3985, e-mail lindalee@tir.com, web site lindaleeoriginals.com. Serger Rescue Kit, Serger Project Cards, Linda's Serger Labels. Brochure, $1 (refundable with order).

Nancy's Notions, Box 683, Beaver Dam, WI 53916-0683, phone (800) 833-0690, fax (800) 255-8119, web site www.nancysnotions.com. Decorative, serger, monofilament-nylon threads, serger needles, most serger notions, and videos. Free catalog.

Palmer/Pletsch Associates, Box 12046, Portland, OR 97212, phone (800) 728-3784, fax (503) 274-1377, web site www.palmer/pletsch.com. Call or write for ordering information. Perfect Sew stabilizer, needle threader/inserter, decorative threads, serger videos, and workshops.

112 Sewing Supplies Inc., 142 Medford Ave., Patchogue, NY 11772, phone (516) 475-8282. Decorative, serger, monofilament-nylon thread, serger needles and notions, serger parts, and accessory feet. Special orders too. Brochure, $1.

SCS (Sewing & Craft Supply) USA, 9631 N.E. Colfax, Portland, OR 97220, phone (800) 542-4727, fax (503) 252-7280, e-mail scs@madeirathreads.com, web site www.madeirathreads.com/scs. Distributor/wholesaler of decorative, serger, and monofilament-nylon threads, needles, and notions. Free catalog.

Sew-Art International, Box 550, Bountiful, UT 84011, phone (800) 231-ARTS, fax (801) 292-0227. Decorative threads and supplies. Free catalog.

Sewing Emporium, 1079 Third Avenue, Suite B, Chula Vista, CA 91910, phone (619) 420-3490, fax (619) 420-4002. Serger accessories, feet, and notions. Catalog, $4.95 (refundable with order).

Speed Stitch, 3113 Broadpoint Drive, Harbor Heights, FL 33983, phone (800) 874-4115, fax (941) 743-4634. Many threads, including all Sulky rayon, plus metallic and invisible thread, Thread Palette, some serger notions. Catalog, $3 (refundable with order).

Stitch n Craft Supply, 5634 W. Meadowbrook, Phoenix, AZ 85031, phone (800) 279-1995, fax or local phone (602) 846-0300, e-mail stitch.craft@mcione.com. Annual subscription/membership fee $25 (includes extensive product sheet binder and home pattern catalogs). Great discounts on serger notions, books, and patterns.

The Sewing Place, Box 111446, Campbell, CA 95011, order phone (800) 587-3937, information and fax (408) 252-8445, web site www.thesewingplace.com. Good selection of household needles, some serger notions (including Crocus Cloth) and a serger video. Free price list.

Treadleart, 25834 Narbonne Ave., Lomita, CA 90717, phone (310), 534-5122, fax (310) 534-8372, e-mail treadleart@treadleart.com, web site www.treadleart.com. Most serger notions and feet, plus variety of threads. Catalog updates $3 (refundable with purchase).

Web of Thread, 1410 Broadway, Paducah, KY 42001, phone (502) 575-9700, fax (502) 575-0904, web site www.webofthread.com. Nearly all decorative threads and yarns, some serger notions. Catalog $3.

YLI Corp., 161 West Main St., Rock Hill, SC 29730, phone (800) 296-8139, fax (803) 985-3106. Variety of serger notions, all-purpose and decorative threads and the original Woolly Nylon. Free brochure.

Sewing machine companies also offer their own specific decorative threads (Elna's Ribbon Thread™, New Home's Janome, and Pfaff's Mez Alcazar, for example), available through their respective dealers. Ask for them at your local dealer. For referral information, see page 54.

BONUS! Serger Specialists
Pattern Companies

The following pattern companies (most knit-sewing specialists) offer patterns with a serging orientation, but the designs are not limited to serging.

Great Copy Patterns, Box 085329, Racine, WI 53408, phone (414) 632-2660, fax (414) 632-0152. Ready-to-wear-inspired designs for serging and conventional sewing. Send SASE for free brochure.

Kwik Sew Pattern Co., 3000 Washington Ave. N., Minneapolis, MN 55411, phone (888) KWIK-SEW, fax (612) 521-1662, e-mail info@kwiksew.com, web site www.kwiksew.com. More than 800 patterns, including knit-oriented designs for serging and conventional sewing. Call for location of dealer nearest you, or mail-order information. Or, send $5 post-paid for a home pattern catalog of the complete line of Kwik Sew patterns.

Linda Lee Originals, 2480 Riniel Road, Lennon, MI 48449, phone (810) 621-4665, fax (810) 621-3985, e-mail lindalee@tir.com, web site lindaleeoriginals.com. Easy-to-make designs focusing on decoratively serged garments and decor, including serger-piecework. Brochure, $1 (refundable with order).

Stretch & Sew Inc., Box 25306, Tempe, AZ 85285-5306, phone (800) 547-7717, fax (602) 966-1914, e-mail stretchsew@worldnet.att.net, web site stretch-and-sew.com. Designs superbly suited to serging. Call for dealer nearest you or mail-order information.

Also refer to the advertising in nationally distributed sewing publications such as **Butterick Home Catalog**, **McCall's Pattern — Sewing's Fashion Magazine**, **Sew News**, **Threads**, and **Vogue Pattern**.

Index

Index

Index

Win a Free Subscription or Video!

Please complete and return this page (photocopies accepted) as soon as possible to the address below. We'll choose several respondents randomly and award each a **FREE one-year subscription** to **Sew News** or a **FREE copy of The Ultimate Serger Answer Guide video** (with **Nancy Zieman** and **Gail Brown**). Send to: **The Ultimate,** P.O. Box 838, Aberdeen, WA 98520.

We Invite You to Talk Back!

We've enjoyed compiling information, researching problems, and testing techniques to prepare The Ultimate Serger Answer Guide for you. Now it's your turn to talk to us. Please fill out the following survey, then jot down your thoughts about this book, specifics about your personal serging endeavors, and any additional serging questions.

We'll do our best to address your questions through various means: revised editions of this book, serging/sewing publications (such as Sew News), on-line computer services, television appearances, seminars, and future books.

Please Rate The Ultimate Serger Answer Guide

	Excellent	Good	Fair	Poor
Content				
Ease/Clarity of Directions				
Charts				
Photography				
Illustrations				

◆ What do you like best about this book?_____

◆ What do you like least about this book?_____

◆ Additional comments: _____

◆ Serging questions/problems not addressed in this book: _____

_____

◆ How did you find out about this book?_____

I own____ (number of) sergers. Serger brand(s)/model(s)_____

I serge for business____ pleasure____ both ____. I serge ___(number of) hours per week.

My serging is mainly utilitarian____decorative____both____. I purchased this book at _____

We need the following information for sending free awards (see above):

Name:_____   Address:_____

City/State/Zip Code:_____   Phone: _____

Fax:_____   E-Mail address(es):_____

If I win, I prefer (circle one): the **Sew News** subscription or **The Ultimate Serger Answer Guide** video.

Thank you! Your comments will help us produce better, reader-friendly publications.

Interested in ordering additional copies of *The Ultimate Serger Answer Guide*?
Call Krause Publications toll-free at (800) 258-0929 for ordering information.